seventeen
ULTIMATE GUIDE TO
COLLEGE

Everything You Need to Know to Walk Onto Campus and *Own* It!

ANN SHOKET &
THE EDITORS OF *seventeen*

PUBLISHED
by

RUNNING PRESS
PHILADELPHIA · LONDON

Hi from Ann! 6
By Ann Shoket, *Seventeen* Editor-in-Chief

HI FROM ANN!

This is it—the moment you've spent so much time preparing for! What will it really be like when you finally step onto the campus of your dream college? You've imagined your cool roommate and the hot guys who will live down the hall in your dorm. You have spent hours on Pinterest pinning décor ideas for your dorm room and have mentally planned all the late-night hangouts with the new friends you will meet. It's fun to imagine and reimagine all the amazing ways your life is going to change once you get to college. It's going to be epic!

But those college fantasies can get a little murky when you're faced with the reality of living alone for the first time. College can get complicated: How will you know which guys are cool (and which are creepers)? What if your roommate turns out to be the worst? And what is that smell in the caf?!?

That's where *Seventeen* comes in. This book is packed with the best advice from girls who have been total college newbies and figured out how to ace every party, date, sorority event, and social situation. They know exactly how to make your roommate love you (or how to keep the peace if that's never going to happen). They can tell you where to find the hot guys and the telltale signs of the dudes who will be a complete drain on your fun. They even know the best stuff to eat in the caf and how to make *your* room the place where everyone on your floor will want to hang out.

Your college experience is going to be every drop of crazy-delicious fun that you've always hoped it would be. With the advice in this book, you can skip every rookie error and walk onto campus on day one like you're a total pro. Who's that confident chick? You are!

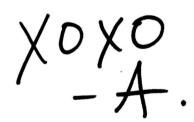

READY, SET... COLLEGE!

everything to do, pack & know before you go!

Starting college might seem ages away, but before you know it, you'll be decorating your dorm room and scoping out cute guys in the caf. Instead of using these next few weeks to obsess about what your life will be like when you get to campus, spend them setting yourself up for four years of awesomeness. Take it from girls who have been there—packing right, planning well, and learning the lingo so you don't look like a newbie are key to having the best college experience possible. Here's your crash course.

COUNTDOWN to college!

The summer isn't just for hanging poolside with your BFFs. This is everything you need to do before you start your freshman year. Ready, set, go!

1 Get a fun summer job.

Pick up as many work shifts as you can, because you'll need lots of cash in college to cover all those midnight study snacks, textbooks, and nights out.

2 Follow your college newspaper on Twitter.

You'll be the girl in the know during the first week of class, so you'll score instant cred!

3 Learn one microwave-friendly recipe.

After dorm food, you'll be craving something—anything!—homemade.

4 Call your roommate.

Figure out what each of you will be bringing. There's no need for you to have two microwaves or refrigerators—especially since space could be extremely tight.

5 Check out public transit.
Find out whether or not it's worth it to have a car at your new school—or if newbies are even allowed to have one. Parking on some college campuses can be nearly impossible… or just really expensive!

6 Make up with anyone you're fighting with.
You don't want to be dealing with lingering drama while you're trying to make a fresh start in college. It will just hold you back from meeting all these amazing new people.

7 Download Skype or Google Hangout.
Add one to your computer if you haven't already, and tell all your friends to do same. Then set up a time each week where you can all log in and video chat. It will transport you back home for 30 minutes!

8 Invest in a dress.
Stick with a black shift (no cleavage!) that can look fancy enough for a job interview or casual enough for hanging out, depending on your accessories.

Make it an LBD!

9 Write a letter to yourself.
List the things you want to accomplish in college. Seal it in an envelope and reread it at the end of the semester to see how far you've come!

10 Rethink your phone plan.
You'll be reaching out a lot to new friends on campus, plus your family and friends back home. (You will miss your mom!) Make sure you have a plan with unlimited texts or at least enough to keep you covered—otherwise you can rack up hundreds in extra charges, and there's no room for that in your college budget!

best year EVER!

New friends, fun clubs, hot parties! These girls learned how to make college unforgettable.

BE A SUPER-FAN!

"When I went to my first college football game, every person in the stadium was decked out in school colors—I felt this amazing sense of community. Even if you're not into the whole school spirit thing, trust me: When you're away from home for the first time, it feels good to know you're part of a family!"

—*Brea, University of Missouri*

ROAD-TRIP!

"In college, I had all this new freedom— and I wanted to use it! So one weekend, my friends and I took a spontaneous 10-hour road trip to Washington, D.C. We were the bosses of where we stayed, where we partied, and what adventures we were going to have. Exploring a new city made me realize how many awesome things are ahead!"

—*Jaymie, College of Charleston*

ROCK OUT AT A CONCERT!

"There are so many freebie events for students on campus—my friends and I are already planning to see our favorite band play!"

—*Chloe, DePaul University*

STAND UP!

"College is the first time I've been around people who are extremely outspoken and politically aware. It's made me realize how important it is to have a voice. So when protests broke out on campus over a proposed tuition hike, I had to join the rally. The experience was surreal—I felt like I was taking charge of my life."

—Brinton, University of California, Davis

BRANCH OUT FROM MY BF!

"My boyfriend and I are going to the same college, so we're spending time apart at first to make new friends separately!"

—Cina, James Madison University

GO TO A THEME PARTY!

"I love theme parties, especially when people get totally into dressing up. I'm so ready to pull out my costumes!"

—Katie, Fashion Institute of Technology

SHOP LIKE A BROKE STUDENT!

"I'm definitely hitting up all the thrift shops in town. A girl's got to save—and look cute doing it!"

—Ally, Savannah College of Art and Design

do college
YOUR WAY

The next four years are about being true to you. Decide how you'll handle *big* decisions before you hit campus, like these girls did!

I CAN'T WAIT TO MEET GUYS

...and I'm going to hook up!

"I don't want to get attached—I'm trying to figure out where I belong. But hooking up can be fun, and college is about freedom! If I see a cutie at a party, I might go for it."

-Ally, Savannah College of Art and Design

...but I'm not going all the way!

"My dorm is coed, so my first thought was: Boys! But even though I'll date, I'm not giving up my virginity—sex should be special, and waiting helps avoid drama."

-Jasmine, California State University, Sacramento

I WANT TO PARTY

...since it's a big part of college!

"I don't need alcohol to have a good time, but I'm open to drinking at parties. I think it's a fun way to meet people—well, as long as you're not blackout drunk."

-Jennifer, University of Central Florida

...but I'm going to do it sober!

"I thought college would make me more open to drinking. But after seeing how sloppy some people get, I know it's not for me. I still go out, and nobody has judged me one bit!"

-Lesley, University of Tampa

MY HS BOYFRIEND & I

...broke up before school!

"If we stayed together, I felt like I wouldn't enjoy all the new experiences at college. I've already hung out with so many people I might not have met if I'd been worrying about a BF back home!"

-Claire, University of Virginia

...are doing the LDR thing!

"I swore I'd never have a BF in college—but there's something about him that I can't let go of! He's three hours away, but I know I always have someone to turn to."

-Devan, Bucknell University

crazy college

#1
Your dorm room will be small and cramped, like a jail cell.

TRUTH:

"It depends on the school, but my dorm is awesome. It's a five-person suite with a lot of closet space and a giant bathroom that's nicer than the one at my parents' house. Apparently at some colleges, you have to share a bathroom with the entire floor. I don't think I could do that!"

–Alexandra, Chaminade University of Honolulu

#2
Cafeteria food is so gross, all you'll want to eat is ramen.

TRUTH:

"The food is better than I expected—especially compared with high school! Our dining hall has a made-to-order sandwich bar, sushi, and even a mini Starbucks. There are also kiosks around campus, like in the library, where you can buy snacks with your meal plan."

–Ricza, Buffalo State College

#3
College parties are raging every night of the week.

TRUTH:

"Sure, there are some massive frat parties, but I was at one 'party' where we were all crammed in a dorm room and played old-school Nintendo games! Even though MSU has a reputation for being a big party school, most days of the week, it's not like that at all."

–Jessica, Michigan State University

MYTHS

This will be one of the best times of your life. But before you get to campus, know that these rumors are total BS.

#4

You schedule your classes so you can sleep in and have long weekends.

TRUTH:

"I haven't met anyone whose schedule was that flexible. Certain classes are offered only at certain times—I couldn't avoid a 9 A.M. science lab on Friday no matter how much I tried. And I have a friend who has to take a five-hour class. School is school!"

—Bernadette, University of California, Berkeley

#5

If you commute to campus, you miss out on the "college experience."

TRUTH:

"As a commuter, I don't have the 'dorm lifestyle,' but I still do tons of stuff on campus. Plus, everyone has time to kill between classes, so it's easy to ask someone to grab coffee. Personally, I don't mind traveling to school. I think it's preparing me for the real world."

—Arianna, Marymount Manhattan College

#6

You'll never get homesick at school… like, never.

TRUTH:

"I couldn't wait to be on my own—then I missed my mom and dog so much, I cried for days. I had to admit that it takes time to adjust, no matter how independent you are."

—Esther, New York University

make a GOOD first impression

Your future roommate and other incoming freshmen will look you up on Twitter, Facebook, Instagram—pretty much wherever you post. This is how to make a zillion new "friends" the right way.

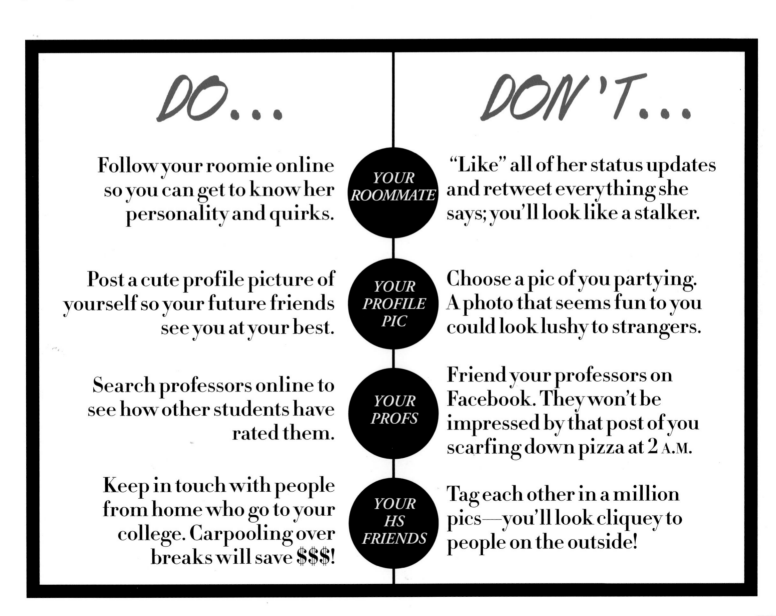

DO...

YOUR ROOMMATE
Follow your roomie online so you can get to know her personality and quirks.

YOUR PROFILE PIC
Post a cute profile picture of yourself so your future friends see you at your best.

YOUR PROFS
Search professors online to see how other students have rated them.

YOUR HS FRIENDS
Keep in touch with people from home who go to your college. Carpooling over breaks will save $$$!

DON'T...

YOUR ROOMMATE
"Like" all of her status updates and retweet everything she says; you'll look like a stalker.

YOUR PROFILE PIC
Choose a pic of you partying. A photo that seems fun to you could look lushy to strangers.

YOUR PROFS
Friend your professors on Facebook. They won't be impressed by that post of you scarfing down pizza at 2 A.M.

YOUR HS FRIENDS
Tag each other in a million pics—you'll look cliquey to people on the outside!

pack like a
SMARTIE

You already have bedding, towels, and a laptop—but don't forget to add these other college essentials!

1 sleeping bag
Your BFF from home will thank you when she crashes with you for a weekend!

2 whiteboard
Everybody hangs one on the outside of her door so people can write messages to each other. Tip: Tie the marker to a piece of ribbon so it doesn't get lost—or "borrowed"!

3 shower caddy
You'll need a place to put your soaps, shampoo, and razor—especially if you share a bathroom with your whole floor.

4 bathing suit
You'll be glad you remembered it when your floormates organize a game of volleyball at the pool or a frat invites you and your friends over to hang in its hot tub!

5 ID holder

Store your school ID card in a cute holder—you don't want to be carrying the generic case from the campus bookstore.

7 one nice outfit

You don't need a whole fancy wardrobe—just one dressier look for the occasional formal.

8 tons of underwear

You need enough pairs to get by from when you *say* you'll do your laundry to when you'll *actually* do it—two weeks later.

6 rain gear

One wet walk to class in your new leather flats and you'll be wishing you had brought a pair of rubber boots and an umbrella!

10 headphones

Your roomie may be tons of fun, but come study time, you'll wish you could just tune her out!

9 cute pajamas

Pack pj's that you're not embarrassed to be seen in—especially if you're living on a coed floor.

should it
STAY OR GO?

Debating over whether to bring it?
Take your cues from some experienced packers.

DO BRING...

A BIKE
It's a fun way to get around campus, and you'll get a workout on your way to class!

YOUR WHEELS

DECORATIONS
Dorm rooms have ugly cinder-block walls—hanging decals and posters will make them way less boring!

YOUR KEEPSAKES

WALKABLE SHOES
You'll be walking everywhere—so pack a few pairs of cute flats and sneakers.

YOUR STYLE

DON'T BRING...

YOUR CAR
You'll save on gas *and* insurance—and you won't be tempted to drive home when you're a little homesick.

A GAZILLION PICTURES FROM HOME
You're going to be making a lot of new memories in college—leave room for those!

EVERY NECKLACE YOU OWN
You'll never feel like going all out for an A.M. class. Just bring a few!

TAKE HER ADVICE!

"Make sure you unpack and organize your dorm room before classes start. Rummaging through all the mess in my room to find my keys made me 10 minutes late to my first class!"

-Mary, University of Florida

WHEN YOU'RE SCOPING OUT CAMPUS
Don't get lost! No need to be the newbie with a map. Before classes start, do a dry run so you don't seem dorky trying to figure out where the heck you're going.

get settled STAT!

With these insider-y tips, your college life will be a blast from day one. Read up now to get a head start at making yourself at home on campus!

When you're super-hungry

Eat the best pizza! Pizza is basically the main food group in college, so ask an upperclassman where the most delish slices are served.

When you want a good party

Follow frats on Twitter! A lot of frats post when they're having cool events, so you'll have the up-to-the-minute deets on where to go.

When it's girls' night

Dive into your candy stash! You'll want to have one—it gives you that little extra jolt of energy to fuel your late-night blab fest. Keep an emergency drawer full of Sour Patch Kids and Skittles.

When you're feeling daring

Join a rando club. The next four years are about discovering new things— and kooky clubs like Quidditch or sky-diving (yup, they exist!) are all about pushing your limits and having a blast.

When you're tailgating

Rock a team T-shirt! You don't have to be into sports, but showing up to a game in your college's swag will instantly make you feel more connected to your campus!

When you want to meet cute guys

Buddy up with your BGF! Being friends with that funny guy from class is like having a built-in wingman—he's the key to finding where the hotties hang.

When you first move in

Prop your door wide open! Your hallmates will peek in to see how your room stacks up, giving you the perf opportunity to chat and make new friends.

5 PEOPLE
you're guaranteed to meet on campus

There are a few characters who seem to be at *every* college. Real girls tell you who to look out for.

THE CLASS SNACKER

" There's one guy who eats basically a full meal during class. The crunching and slurping are so disruptive! Professors might be lax about eating in class, but it's not okay to show up with the entire contents of the cafeteria! "

—Aliyyah, *University of Pennsylvania*

THE ORIENTATION CREEPER

" I met a girl at orientation who was nice but then immediately added me on Facebook and started following me everywhere. The thing is, you meet so many people during the first week that everyone is relaxed about it. When someone instantly comes on too strong, you know to rule them out! "

—Katie, *University of North Carolina*

THE GYM TOOLBAG

" One time this overly tanned, muscled guy at the gym tried to ask me out by asking me if I'd ever 'really seen the city of Eau Claire.' It was such a line! Beware of any gym rat who seems a little too smooth—he uses the gym as his personal pickup spot. Ew! "

—Carly, *University of Wisconsin–Eau Claire*

THE R.A. WANNABE

❝ A girl in my dorm acts as if she's in charge—and she's not. She declared my outfit 'inappropriate' at a party, and she rats out people who have guys in their room past curfew. It totally breaks the college code—everyone knows you don't sell out other students. **❞**

—Olivia, Mount Mary University

THE CAFETERIA FASHIONISTA

❝ There's a girl I notice in the caf because she always looks perfect—even during finals! I'm jealous of how cute she is, but when everyone else is wearing sweats, it just seems like a little too much effort! **❞**

—Veronica, Rice University

how to SPEAK COLLEGE

Get ready to hear these words constantly. Study up now, and everyone will think you know what's going on from the first day.

"DORMCEST"

(n): Hooking up with someone in your dorm—can lead to awkward run-ins if things fizzle.

"BREAKS-GIVING"

(n): Refers to the time of year—around Thanksgiving—when many freshmen dump their long-distance high school sweethearts because they're having more fun in college! Also called "Turkey Dump."

"JUNGLE JUICE"

(n): A punch served at parties (usually in a giant cooler) that tastes like fruit juice but is packed with alcohol. Warning: It's scary strong.

"FRACKET"

(n): A cheap jacket you wear only to frat parties—if it gets stolen or stomped on, who cares?

"SEXILED"

(adj.): Refers to being "exiled" from your room because your roommate is hooking up and needs total privacy. Example: "I had to sleep in the study lounge last night because I got sexiled."

"HIGHLIGHTER PARTY"

(n): A party with a black light where everyone wears white and writes on each other with highlighters. By the end, you're glowing!

THE POWER NAP
The world's greatest invention. Twenty minutes, in between classes. Trust us—it's life-changing.

COLLEGE SECRETS

(NO ONE TELLS YOU!)

There are unspoken rules of college that most girls figure out the hard way. Consider yourself lucky.

LATE-NIGHT PIZZAS
are a rite of passage—but if you indulge too many nights in a row, they'll make you feel like the greasy doughballs they are.

RED BULL
will totally help you power through exams—but an overload will make you too jittery to type straight!

THEME PARTY
Never go to a theme party without a costume. Togas, tiaras, leis, or anything out of the ordinary suddenly turn into amazing props to flirt with.

FLIP-FLOPS
are a *must.* Communal college bathrooms are a fungus fest!

give yourself a
MUCH-NEEDED BREAK

It's easy to feel overwhelmed thinking about what life will be like on campus. (You're not the only one stressing!) But take a breath and learn from these real girls who survived first semester.

It's okay to be alone.

"The first week of school, I bought my books, supplies, and groceries all on my own—without resorting to talking on my cell the whole time. I used to feel weird doing stuff by myself, but now that I have to, I like being able to do my own thing."

–Meghan, Pacific Northwest College of Art

If you feel intimidated at first, that's normal!

"In high school, I was the all-star. But in college, it's like you take all the best athletes, the popular girls, the pretty girls—and you put them in one place. I couldn't stop comparing myself. It made me feel inferior. But I realized that I need to figure out who I want to be."

–Anique, Howard University

Friendships aren't always measured in years.

"When one of my new friends broke up with her boyfriend, I was the one she came to. It didn't matter to me that I'd never met the guy or that we hadn't known each other for long. In college, everyone needs a new support system, so you bond fast with people who 'get' you."

–Rachel, Columbia University

Make time for yourself.

"In college, there is so much to do all the time. I found myself getting no sleep—and then passing out during lectures. I started getting stressed and even felt depressed. Finally on a Saturday night, I couldn't take it anymore—so I stayed in. You'll rarely find time for yourself in college, so you have to make it."

–Holly, Purdue University

You can change your mind.

"Before I left for college, I made this big decision not to date because I was afraid it would be a distraction. But then I developed feelings for one of my very best guy friends. I realized it was okay to change my mind, as long as I stayed true to my core values."

–Katie, Texas A&M University

LEAVE these

Getting ready for your first year is a big deal. These girls

"I've heard that in college, you're really on your own—but between dorm life, classes, and the dining hall, I'm never actually alone. I love how friendly and social everyone is."

-Brittany, University of Pittsburgh

"It's totally fine if you don't drink! I've met tons of cool people through Facebook, orientation, and other functions who like to party sober."

-Lauren, DePaul University

"There's still **so much gossip** about who hooked up with this guy who's taken, or who picked a fight with her friends. The difference is that I'm over it. **Catty girls exist everywhere,** but if you stop paying so much attention, you can have a fresh start."

-Berkley, University of Mary Washington

worries behind

will make sure your head is in the right place!

"When I was applying to schools, I had **a serious boyfriend** and was worried about moving away from him. But now I'm single, and **meeting new people** is so much fun! Making guy friends is definitely something to look forward to."

–Janessa, University of California, San Diego

"I was worried my new friends would judge me for being a virgin, because I thought I was the only one. But when it came out, my friends—guys and girls—were impressed. Once I stopped hiding it, I met a bunch of other girls who are virgins, too. College brings together all sorts of people with different views!"

–Jenna, American University

"Going to college is less scary than you'd think, because everyone is in the same shoes. No one knows anybody—so it's easy to make friends."

–Holly, Purdue University

"Everyone's parents are emotional and embarrassing when they move their child in—no need to stress about Mom's tearful hugs!"

–Rachel, Columbia University

"Before I got to campus, I was worried about meeting new people. But living on your own helps you feel more confident, and now I'm best friends with the majority of the girls on my floor!"

ASK AN INSIDER!

Ariel Kellogg, Fashion Institute of Technology

MAJOR:
Advertising/marketing communication.

GO-TO DORM FOOD:
Veggie burgers. They take only two minutes in the microwave.

BEST PLACE TO STUDY:
It's cliché but the library. It's quiet, and no one bothers you!

I TOTALLY DIDN'T NEED:
Half of my wardrobe. I overpacked!

TRICK TO GET A GUY'S ATTENTION IN CLASS:
Know the material. Intelligence is a beautiful thing.

FAVORITE PARTY LOOK:
Red lipstick pulls together whatever you're wearing.

EASIEST WAY TO SAVE $$$:
Make your own coffee—all those three-dollar splurges add up!

CURE FOR HOMESICKNESS:
Skyping with my parents—trust me, you will miss yours!

GOING-OUT BUDGET:
I've got bills to pay, and books are expensive. I try to keep it to $20 a weekend.

FUTURE DREAM JOB:
I would love to design textiles or own my own thrift store.

FAVORITE THEME-PARTY COSTUME:
I went to an "alien party" and wore my hair in three buns.

WHERE TO MEET GUYS ON CAMPUS:
If you find a place, let me know—my school is mostly girls!

HOW TO BE BFFs WITH YOUR ROOMMATE:
Dress up and go out. It doesn't matter where—the whole getting-dolled-up process is a good way to bond and borrow each other's clothes.

chapter two

LOVE YOUR DORM LIFE!

make your roommate ♥ you!

You haven't been this excited—and nervous!—to meet someone ever. It makes sense: Hopefully your roommate is the girl you'll share everything with, from late-night snacks to stories about the guy you're crushing on. You want her to be the person in all your Instagram pics now—and ideally your friend for life. Awesome? Yes! But it's also a lot of pressure. Here's how to deal with the good stuff, the drama, and your new room!

be the BEST roomie ever!

You're sharing a small space with this girl for a whole year—of course you want her to think she hit the roommate jackpot! Use these tips to start off right.

DO...

BEFORE YOU MEET

Call her to see what music she's into and where she shops. Look for ways you're alike, and appreciate how you're different. Also, decide who will bring what for the room!

ON MOVE-IN DAY

Go out for pizza and discuss how you each feel about drinking, guests, and noise. Setting rules will prevent fights later. (Turn to page 48 for help with this convo.)

TWO WEEKS IN

Give her some space. Plan a movie night with her once a week—but go out with other people too. This will give you both a chance to make new friends.

DON'T...

BEFORE YOU MEET

Set ground rules right off the bat—why introduce conflict before you even know her? Besides, she's got plenty of time to learn about your quirks.

ON MOVE-IN DAY

Call dibs on the bigger closet. Otherwise she'll be irritated from the start and it will be twice as hard to win her over.

TWO WEEKS IN

Talk about what she does in the privacy of your room. It will get back to her, and she'll be pissed. If there's an issue, meet her at a café and gently talk to her.

easy ways to

"For a while, it seemed like my roommate and I wouldn't be friends—we didn't have a lot in common. Then I went through a serious breakup. She was the first one to bring out the ice cream and tissues, and that unexpected kindness made us best friends!"

—Brianna, Elon University

"My roommate and I bonded by making Nutella sandwiches to befriend the cute guys on our floor. It worked out really well for us—and the guys, too!"

—Selena, Johns Hopkins University

"My roomie and I decided to go out to this block party near campus. We took a million photos together, and she got this one shot of me falling down a hill in front of at least 200 people. We both thought it was hilarious, and after that, we were best friends! All we needed was one night of silliness."

—Natalie, University of Hawaii

bond...FAST!

sometimes it takes the right moment for things to click.

"We clicked decorating our room! My roomie had a **Red Hot Chili Peppers poster,** which led us to talk about our similar taste in music. And I had two prints of New York, which got us talking about **the places we had traveled to that summer.** Those posters turned out to be great conversation starters!"

-Emily, The College of William & Mary

"Just by luck, I got roomed with a girl who loves organic foods! We made it our mission to try a different organic restaurant every week, which made us super-close. You just need one thing in common to start—once you find that, the rest is easy!"

-Christine, University of Florida

"We found out we're both obsessed with funny cat videos. That's all it took!"

-Lizzie, James Madison University

"I knew we were going to be BFFs when we decided to stay in one night, watch chick flicks, and order takeout. So cliché, but that night really brought us closer!"

-Camille, Pennsylvania State University

your roommate
RULE BOOK!

You just moved out of your parents' house, so pretty much the last thing you want are rules.
But you and your roommate *do* need to create guidelines so you don't get on each other's nerves!
These tricks will keep both of you sane.

1 Remember it's a room for two.

If you get serious with that frat guy you met in the caf, chances are nobody will be happier with your BF/GF status than your roomie. Just don't make your room the de facto hangout spot—she signed up for one roomie, not two!

2 Ask first.

"Borrowing" body wash or printer ink seems like no biggie, but that stuff adds up fast! Unless you went halfsies on paying for it, get permission!

3 Text her if you're bringing a guy over.

If you spring a visitor on her, she'll feel like you're not respecting that it's her space too.

4 Hold the calls.

For phone convos longer than a few minutes, take it outside of your room. It's annoying for your roommate to listen to you babbling when she's trying to study—and you'll appreciate it when you're the one hitting the books.

5 Give *her* way a chance.

Always keep an open mind. You may end up loving that music, food, or quirky poster of hers that you initially thought was weird.

6 Keep mornings quiet.

This means no hitting snooze a million times or constantly opening and closing the door. Drape your outfit over your chair the night before an early-morning class so you're not (loudly) digging through your closet either!

7 Let little things go.

If she occasionally stumbles homes at 4 A.M. and wakes you up, give her a pass. (You'll probably have those moments too!) Confront her only if she's being inconsiderate on a regular basis. You can ask your RA for advice on how to talk to your roommate about it, or have her mediate a discussion.

8 Schedule some solo time.

Instead of doing everything together, have a time each week when you'll go to the gym or library and ask your roomie to do the same—then you can both count on a few hours alone in the room.

9 Don't go MIA for too long.

You'll freak her out! If you're not coming back that night or if you go away for a weekend, tell her beforehand or send a quick text to let her know, so she's not worried.

10 Respect bedtime.

If one of you turns in for an early class, the overhead light should go out and a desk lamp and headphones should go on.

what's your
ROOMMATE-TIONSHIP?

**There are all different kinds of roommate scenarios.
Figure out your sitch!**

ROOM-MANCE

Roomies who love each other so much, they're attached at the hip.
See also: bromance, romance, BFFs

this is you if... your roommate is in every one of your pics and status updates. You have inside jokes that nobody else understands. You eat almost every meal together and can finish each other's sentences.

HOW-DO-YOU-DOERS

You're not BFFs, but you're polite.
See also: acquaintances, people who don't steal each other's stuff

this is you if... you don't really hang out, but when you see each other on campus, you're friendly. This can actually be a great scenario—you have a peaceful living situation *and* are pushed to make new friends.

ENE-MATES

Roommates who don't like each other.
See also: people who walk by each other in the quad and don't make eye contact

this is you if... your roommate doesn't respect you or your space. If you're constantly being "sexiled" or your roomie makes you uncomfortable, talk to your RA about switching rooms.

MIXED BAG

Sometimes, you're barely speaking, and other times, you're close.
See also: roller-coaster roommates

this is you if... you're not besties, but you can have fun together. Sometimes you might stay up all night talking; other times, you go days barely seeing each other. As long as there's no drama, that's totally okay!

HOW TO DEAL...
if your roomie GOES CRAZY!

You'll probably get along. But if by chance you get roomed with a total nut job, try this advice from girls who have been there, handled that.

OMG!
THE SERIAL KLEPTO

"A girl I know had a roommate who stole her clothes, shoes, and food. She even moved my friend's TV to her side of the room without asking if it was okay! My friend confronted her, but it didn't help. Finally, she went to her RA for assistance."

–Veronica, Rice University

RUDE!
THE CHRONIC COMPLAINER

"My suitemate has no idea how to live with other people. She hangs up crazy notes bitching about everything. One time, she posted a note complaining that someone stole one of her dishes—then realized she'd left it in the refrigerator! I just roll my eyes at her instead of getting caught up in the drama."

–Bria, Columbia College Chicago

UGH!
THE LOVESICK WHINER

"My friend's roommate cries herself to sleep over missing her boyfriend, refuses to go out on weekends because she Skypes him, and even said she's too upset to shower! My friend tried to pull her out of it, but she realized it's not her job to keep her roomie happy."

–Carly, University of Wisconsin–Eau Claire

LEARN FROM MY MISTAKE AND SET GROUND RULES!

"I knew something was wrong when my roommate said, 'I can tell I'm not going to like you by the end of the year.' Great. She mocked me while I talked on the phone and called me a *sorostitute* (*sorority* + *prostitute*) because I rushed. Every day was a new kind of torture. We'd never set ground rules, and I was afraid of confronting her, so I let her walk all over me. Only after I'd moved in with a new roommate did I realize I should have stood up for myself. If I had, my freshman year would have been completely different!

-Margaret, *The College of William & Mary*

CREATE A
DRAMA-FREE ZONE

When you're sharing such a tiny space, you're bound to have a fight or two. This is how real girls got over their first dose of roomie drama.

DON'T PICK SIDES

" I live with three other girls, and there came a point where it seemed like it was always two against two. After weeks of tension, we finally sat down and talked. Now we make sure to confront problems as soon as they come up! "

–Cameron, 20, Virginia Tech

TRY A RANDOM ACT OF KINDNESS

" My roomie became introverted—and I took it personally. Turns out, she was stressed from taking six classes instead of four. When she finally told me, I made her a wall of photos of things she loved to make her feel better. It worked! "

–Amanda, Barnard College

BE UP-FRONT ABOUT GUY TIME

" My BF was coming into town and my roommate wasn't comfortable having him in the room. After I told her it was important to me to see him, we made a schedule of 'boyfriend-over' and 'boyfriend-less' times so we could both have space. "

–Andrea, 21, Virginia Tech

CLEAR THE AIR

" For weeks, I didn't say anything when my roomie ignored her alarm clock every morning—then one day I snapped at her. She was annoyed because I hadn't told her sooner. I learned it's better to speak up than bottle up anger! "

–Jamie, The College of New Jersey

55

your AWESOME room essentials

Finally, it's time to cute-ify your space! Don't forget these 10 must-haves when you're getting stuff for your new room.

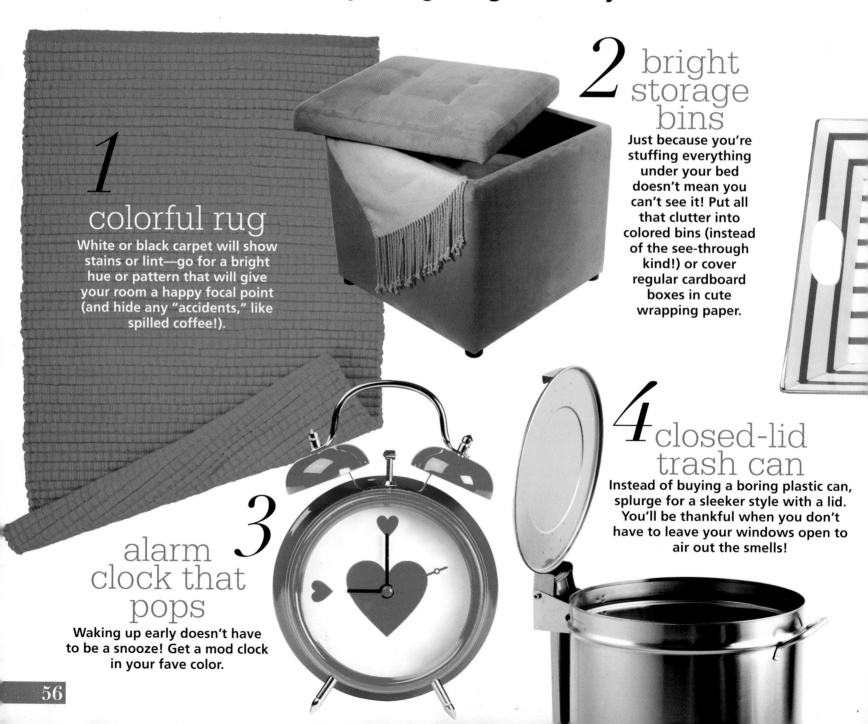

1 colorful rug

White or black carpet will show stains or lint—go for a bright hue or pattern that will give your room a happy focal point (and hide any "accidents," like spilled coffee!).

2 bright storage bins

Just because you're stuffing everything under your bed doesn't mean you can't see it! Put all that clutter into colored bins (instead of the see-through kind!) or cover regular cardboard boxes in cute wrapping paper.

3 alarm clock that pops

Waking up early doesn't have to be a snooze! Get a mod clock in your fave color.

4 closed-lid trash can

Instead of buying a boring plastic can, splurge for a sleeker style with a lid. You'll be thankful when you don't have to leave your windows open to air out the smells!

6
pretty throw pillows
Nothing spruces up your space faster than adding a few pillows to your bed. Mix stripes with polka dots or other patterns so you don't look too matchy-matchy.

not-a-desk lamp
Forget putting some metal office lamp in your study space (boring), and get a fun lamp you'd normally put on a side table or shelf. It will look way cuter and still do the job!

5
something monogrammed
Towels, pillows, coffee cups, wall art—say "I live here!" with your initials!

7
stash-anything tray
It's easy for all the little stuff to clutter up your desk, so plop your jewelry, spare change, keys, mail, whatever, in here and you'll have a go-to spot for the things you're always losing.

8

9
funky speakers
Your laptop speakers are fine when you're doing homework alone, but snag a speaker set for when you have friends over. For $20 or less, you can have a dance party with your hallmates and actually hear the music!

10
sleek photo hanger
Don't waste money on frames! Hang your fave pics and cards from a wire using paper clips, and you've got a live Instagram you can touch!

CHOOSE YOUR
VIBE!

It's your first real space—so make sure it feels like you! Decorate for your style with these ideas.

1. JAM OUT
Hit up the vintage record store and play up your individuality by framing old album covers and concert posters!

2. MIX UP BEDDING
Style your bed like you would an outfit—using different prints and colors makes it more personal.

3. DRESS THE WINDOWS
Layers of curtains make a room feel more like home—plus, they block the view of those gross guys across the courtyard!

4. SHOW OFF YOUR STYLE
Dorm rooms can have teeny-tiny closets. Make the best of it by turning your cutest clothing into a design statement with a hanging rack.

It can double as a room divider when you want some privacy!

CHIC SOPHISTICATE

1. LINE 'EM UP

Add some serious style to blah dorm walls by applying black-stripe wall decals in a vertical pattern. Bonus: They will peel right off when you're ready to move out!

2. FRAME YOUR BED

You can create the illusion of a luxurious canopy (and make your dormmates jealous!) by hanging sheer window panels on either side of your bed.

3. COUCH IT

Make your bed do double-duty as a sofa—center it on the wall and cover it with plush pillows. Then settle in for a long night of gossip.

4. HIT THE FLOOR

An oversize pouf will provide additional comfy seating for guests. (Your new problem: getting friends to leave… .)

5. CREATE ART

Build a gallery-style wall with photos and framed mementos. The graphic print inside this black picture frame is actually a sample of wallpaper!

say that you love me.

YUMMY DORM

SALAD PARFAIT

Take your Tupperware down to the caf and make this cute salad for later! Start with a little vinaigrette on the bottom, then work your way up with lettuce, veggies, and some sort of protein like chicken or beans.

PB SUSHI

Spread peanut butter on a banana, roll it in Rice Krispies for crunch, and dip slices in Nutella to get a hit of sweet!

YO-GO

Keep some Greek yogurt in your fridge—it has more protein and less sugar than the regular kind, so it will fill you up if you're pulling an all-nighter. Mix in sides of granola, honey, almonds, and fresh or dried fruit for more flavor!

EATS!

You'll eat most of your meals in the caf, but keep a few key foods in your room for a quick bite that's way tastier than a bowl of cereal.

VEGGIE + PITA BURGER

Step one: Snag some veggies from the caf or hit up the nearby grocery store. Step two: Microwave a veggie burger right in your dorm. Step three: Stick it all in a pita, and chow down. So much better than the fast food on campus!

SNACK ATTACK!

Fuel your next study session with these better-for-you bites.

SKIP IT: POP-TARTS
PICK IT: RICE KRISPIES TREATS

Pop-Tarts are so high in calories that one pouch is the equivalent of a meal. But a Rice Krispies Treat is mostly airy cereal, with just enough sweetness and crunch to satisfy you.

SKIP IT: DORITOS
PICK IT: CHIPS & SALSA

The powder on Doritos is full of artificial additives! Dip plain corn tortilla chips (they're more natural) in salsa for some low-fat flavor instead.

SKIP IT: OREOS
PICK IT: FIG NEWTONS

Sugar treats can set off more cravings, so you eat too many. But 100% Whole-Grain Fig Newtons have fruit and a little more fiber than Oreos, so you'll fill up faster.

make your room the
PARTY SPOT!

When your room is the coolest place on the floor to hang out, it's a guaranteed way to meet new people.

EASY ACCESS
Always prop open your door so it's easy for floormates to stop in to say hi.

VIEWING PARTY
Invite people over to watch *Catfish* or *The Real Housewives* of wherever—shared guilty pleasures are a fast way to bond!

WHITEBOARD
Hang up an erasable board on your door too, so people can doodle on it or leave messages when you're out.

GET A PET
A cute goldfish will become your floor's mascot. Take a fun poll to pick out his name!

"In a dorm room, there's no real seating, so movie nights include squishing on someone's twin bed and streaming Netflix on a laptop."

–Samantha,
Grinnell College

65

"Don't stress if you aren't best friends with your freshmen roommates! I had two, and they were nice girls, but we just never really got close."

ASK AN INSIDER!

Danai Sabrina Kadzere, Harvard University

MAJOR:
Human evolutionary biology.

COLLEGE MOTTO:
Don't take yourself so seriously! It's okay to screw up sometimes.

DORM-ROOM STYLE:
Girly and pink.

I'M SO GLAD I PACKED:
Glitter pens! Studying organic chem is so much more fun when it glitters.

I TOTALLY DIDN'T NEED:
My 300th pack of college-ruled filler paper.

FAVORITE CAF FOOD:
Cereal and fro-yo.

MOST LIKELY TO CRUSH ON:
Tall handsome nerds!

WORST TEXT I GOT FROM A COLLEGE GUY:
"You're as hot as my girlfriend." *Ummm....*

GO-TO OUTFIT FOR CLASS:
Jeans, cute shirt, loafers.

TOP THING EVERY COLLEGE GIRL NEEDS IN HER CLOSET:
A sweatshirt you can snuggle into during your first all-nighter at the library.

PART-TIME JOB:
I work at the library. It's essential, since I'm financially independent from my parents!

MINUTES SPENT GETTING READY FOR CLASS IN THE A.M.:
Ten—I just put my hair in a ponytail and go.

NUMBER ONE PARTY RULE:
Go out with a friend you trust. Always. Oh, and don't spill your drink on people.

I'M CURRENTLY SAVING FOR:
A place to live after graduation that isn't a cardboard box!

chapter three

MASTER THE GUY SCENE

what college guys *really* think!

It's no secret that one of the best parts of college is that you get to flirt, date, and hook up with whatever cute guy you want—minus the embarrassment of your parents catching you. College guys are a lot more relaxed than the dudes at your high school, and just having flirty fun is way more common than locking down a boyfriend. Now that you're on campus, here's how to navigate the new rules of dating so you know which guys to look out for, what college hookup culture is really like, and most important, how to have a blast (while still protecting your heart!).

4 THINGS
you need to know about dudes in college

It's impossible to know *exactly* what the guy situation will be like before you get to campus, but this is a primer on what you can expect—wherever you're going!

1. THEY'RE CURIOUS

At first, it might feel like every guy just wants to fool around. College is your first taste of freedom—and his, too—so don't hold it against him if he's not into being exclusive. (Just move on to someone else!) Some people will want to settle down in college, but lots like to stay unattached all four years!

2. THEY'RE DRIVEN

Some guys act like all they want out of college is a good time, so it might seem like they want a girl who parties hard. But plenty of college guys have big career goals, and they respect ambitious girls. So stay true to your dreams—it's way more impressive than being awesome at flip cup.

3. THEY'RE BOLD

In high school, people might have been scared to venture outside of their little cliques to make friends. But college is all about meeting people—seriously, everyone is new—and guys embrace this. At a party, in class, even just walking around campus— there are tons of opportunities for guys to approach you and say hi … and they will!

4. THEY'RE POOR

A lot of college guys can't afford fancy dates— they spend their money on things like books, beer, and fraternity dues. But a late-night talk at a diner or pizza and a basketball game on TV can be very romantic. And without the big-night-out hoopla, you really have a chance to focus on whether he's thoughtful, smart, kind, and funny enough to be with you!

7 GUYS
you'll definitely meet on campus

Warning: There will be tons of cool dudes but also some duds. Find out how to suss out your prospects.

THE CUTE ONES

the dorm crush

"I'm dating a guy who lives on the floor below mine. Since I'm always walking around in my pajamas and wearing my glasses and retainers but no makeup, I know he likes me for who I really am."

—Casey, *Indiana University*

the indie cutie

"I thought college life revolved around partying. Then I dated an artsy guy who wasn't into doing what everyone else was doing. We'd explore the city or just hang out and play games."

—Brittany, *University of Pittsburgh*

the perfect BF

"People say that no one in college goes on real dates, but ladies, my boyfriend cooks for me! Don't settle for a guy who never puts in any effort, because there are guys who will!"

—Leceeon, *University of Akron*

THE CREEPY ONES

the undercover player

"This shy guy got close to me with cute texts… then I found out he was sending the same messages to lots of girls! College is a big place— it's easy for guys to play around."

—Sharai, *Fordham University*

the makeout bandit

"At a club, I was dancing with this random guy, and suddenly he was trying to kiss me! Ew! Some college guys act like it's the norm to be forward, so back off if you get weird vibes!"

—Lauren, *DePaul University*

the cocky jock

"College athletes are like celebs—so they're used to getting girls. When I didn't respond to this football guy on Facebook, he freaked and made his status: 'KATIE WRITE ME BACK!'"

—Katie, *Texas A&M University*

THE SNEAKIEST ONE!

"Watch out for the insta-boyfriend! I hit it off with this guy at a party, and for the next few days, we hung out nonstop. Then he totally stopped talking to me. It's like he was into me just because he was lonely—but I actually thought his intensity was real."

–*Megan, Pacific Northwest College of Art*

THE NEW RULES
of dating

Follow this guide to avoid awkward moments—
and snag that guy you've been crushing on!

1 Coffee after class counts as a date.

"Dating in college is super-casual—grabbing coffee after class or watching TV together in one of your dorm rooms can be dating!"

-Katie, *University of North Carolina*

2 Speak up!

"Some college classes are huge, so you have to work to get to know people. My tip: Sit by the hot guys and actually talk to them!"

-Dev'n, *Texas Tech University*

3 Avoid the "down dater" at all costs.

"Watch out for upperclassmen who date *only* freshmen—they tend to assume you're a really easy target. There might be some exceptions, but as a general rule, you should run from them as if they have the plague!"

-Laura, *Appalachian State University*

4 Always say hi to your hookup the day after.

"A friend hooked up with a guy on Friday, and then on Saturday, she realized that her seat at the football game was right next to his! You live, work, and party with the same people—she had to say hi so she wouldn't have to awkwardly avoid him for the next four years!"

—Casi, Stanford University

5 Beware the prebooty text.

"Guys know that girls don't want to be just a booty call—they'll purposefully text you early on, so it's less sketchy when they ask to hook up at the end of the night. Don't fall for it!"

—Morgan, University of Pennsylvania

6 Never assume you're exclusive with a guy.

"I know a guy who is two-timing girls from completely different social circles. College is massive, so those girls may never know about each other. It's best to assume relationships are open unless you discuss otherwise."

—Sarita, Columbia University

7 Introduce your crush to your roommate ASAP.

"If you like him, bring him to your room so he and your roomie can meet. If she's friends with him too, she won't care as much when he drops by your tiny dorm room all the time or sleeps over a few nights a week!"

—Noelia, Wesleyan University

8 Leave a little mystery.

"I met this guy I liked, so I opened up—a lot—even though we had just met. But when he broke up with me just a month later, it hurt that much more since he knew everything about me. Now I know there are things I can wait to share—the guy has to earn my trust!"

—Jenny, Syracuse University

9 Don't hook up with a guy on your floor.

"'Floorcest' is a huge no-no. If the relationship doesn't last, you'll realize all the awkward ways you can run into an ex you practically live with. It's horrible!"

—Berna, University of Southern California

10 Don't limit your options.

"Don't get trapped in 'the college bubble'—new guys are everywhere! Once I danced all night with a local guy I met at an off-campus party, and another time I was shopping when I met a party promoter who went to school nearby. "

—Aliyyah, University of Pennsylvania

SECRETS
that guys wish you knew

You can't read his mind—but now you don't have to! These dudes are filling you in on what they've been thinking all semester.

THEY'RE MORE MATURE NOW

"In high school, if I got into a fight with my girlfriend, I'd just break up with her. I never really cared about the girls I was dating. But now that I'm finding girls I have a deeper connection with, I make a real effort to work through our problems."

–Nicholas, 18

THEY MAKE BETS WITH THEIR FRIENDS

"My friends and I bet on who can talk to more girls. The competition forces me to get over my nerves and just go for it! Then we try to organize a group hangout with the girls we're into. Even though we're competing, we help each other by being wingmen!"

–Jason, 18

THEY PLAY A LITTLE HARD TO GET

"I try to sit near the cutest girl in my class and talk with everyone but her. That way, I'll look really social and she'll want to get my attention really badly."

–Spencer, 20

THEY LIKE WHEN GIRLS GO FOR IT

"I was at a party dancing with a girl—and she asked me to go back to her room! In high school, I think it was easier for girls to get a reputation if they hooked up. But in college, it's NBD."

—Christian, 19

THEY WANT YOU TO APPROACH THEM DURING THE DAY

"Parties bring out the 'fun guys,' but sometimes that's it. The best way to meet the good guys is through class, clubs, and sports. Guys who put effort into those things will put energy into a relationship, too."

—Ryan, 19

THEY GET SPIFFED UP TO IMPRESS YOU

"I get a haircut before classes start to look sharp during the first week. If a new girl thinks I'm attractive when we meet, I'll stay that attractive in her mind when I run into her again!"

—Ernest, 20

THEY WANT YOUR NUMBER "JUST IN CASE"

"I'll sit next to a hot girl and suggest we trade numbers so that if one of us misses class, we can share assignments. It's a great excuse to text her."

—Lane, 19

be a hookup
SMARTIE!

**You want to be the girl all the guys want to hang out with—
not the girl crying because her crush didn't text her back!
Here's how to stay on top of your game so that you can have fun!**

DO...

DON'T...

IN THE BEGINNING

Protect your heart. When you live at school, there's more time to hang out with a guy. You might think you're ready for the next level, but it's best to take things slowly at first.

Expect to be exclusive at first. No-strings-attached hookups are way more common than serious relationships, and most people aren't rushing into a commitment.

IF HE WANTS YOU ALONE

Realize he doesn't care about your dorm. One trick guys use is saying, "I've never been to that dorm! Want to show me?" It's just a slimy move to go back to your place.

Ignore the signs. Inviting you to watch a DVD on his laptop is code for "I want you in my bed so I can make a move." The ultimate sign he's into you is if his room is clean!

IF IT DOESN'T WORK OUT

Be selective. Expect every guy to hit on you—but don't feel like you need to hang out (or hook up) with a dude just because he flirts with you!

Stress over a crummy hookup. Next time you don't hear from a guy, look for clues he's not interested in more, like if he's all over you in two seconds.

"I WENT HOOKUP CRAZY!"

"In high school, I never had a serious boyfriend, and I went off to college really excited to find one. Then the first week of school, I met a guy at a frat party. We hit it off and started hanging out—but I didn't think he was cute, so I never hooked up with him. On the weekends, he'd invite me to frat parties, and I'd flirt with tons of guys. Even though I never planned on hooking up, most nights ended that way. I liked that I was in the guys' inner circle. But after a while, hooking up with so many guys in the same frat made me embarrassed, and it hit me how much I valued my friendship with my guy friend. I tried texting him, but after seeing me hook up with so many of his frat brothers, he stopped answering. The hookups were fun, but they cost me something bigger—now I'm looking for a real relationship."

−Jaclyn, *University of Michigan*

YOUR CUTE CLASSMATE

"It's easy to start talking to the guy who sits next to you—and if things go downhill, there are new classes every 10 weeks!"

—Brinton, University of California, Davis

the HOTTEST
guys on campus
(AND WHERE TO SPOT 'EM!)

You can date anyone in college—so don't waste a second on the losers! These five cuties have way more potential than some drunk dude at a party.

THE SMARTIE JOCK

66 In my dorm, there's this one guy who is famous for his abs, but he's also an athlete who gets really good grades. Talk about the total package. We're all crushing on him! 99

–Melisa, Harvard University

THE CAF CRUSH

66 My friend hooked up with the guy who works in the dining hall— and now he gives her free food all the time! 99

–Mele, University of San Francisco

THE LIBRARY HOTTIE

66 People stake out the same spot every time, so you can make eye contact with a cute guy again and again. My friend met her boyfriend that way! 99

–Yolis, Texas State University

YOUR ROOMMATE'S FRIEND

66 I met my guy through my roommate. If a guy is dropping by your room to see you all the time, it's better if your roommate likes him instead of being completely annoyed! 99

–Jenna, American University

don't be
THAT GIRL

Getting a bad rep can be as easy as one frat-party faux pas. Here, real guys tell you how to win dudes over for the right reasons!

DON'T BE A BUMMER

"I liked this girl, but once we got to talking about goals and dreams, her responses were super-negative. She said she wanted to be a lawyer but that it was too hard and would take too long. I lost interest—I want to be with someone who believes in herself and her future."

—Edam, Syracuse University

DON'T GET TEST-Y

"I saw a girl from my calculus class at a party and she started talking to me about our exam. The last thing I wanted was a reminder that I needed to study the next day! She's cool, but she should have talked to me about something more exciting, like how I did at my last track meet or if I liked the playlist at the party."

—Olu, Bucknell University

DON'T MASS TEXT

"I thought my flirty texting with this girl was our thing. Then I got a text message from her about hanging out, and these replies from other dudes started flashing on my phone. I was part of one big mass text! I felt sort of cheated, and I wondered how much she liked me in the first place."

—Griffin, University of Tampa

DON'T RUSH IT

"After I dropped off a girl I'd been dating for a few weeks, she turned and yelled, 'I love you!' I freaked—I'm glad she cared, but I wish she had waited to say something so important. It made me think she didn't really mean it!"

—Ben, Central Connecticut State University

DON'T EX OBSESS

"I hung out with a girl once and she wouldn't stop talking about her ex. If she missed him so much, she should have hung out with him. Focus on the present—I want to know you're into me, not your last guy!"

—Austin, University of Missouri

85

YIKES!

dating *SCANDALS* you need to avoid

Campus is big...but not that big. Real girls share their juiciest gossip so you know how to protect your rep.

DATING THE TEACHER!

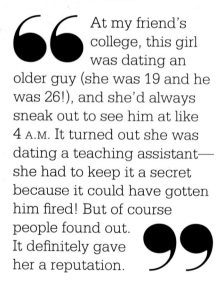

At my friend's college, this girl was dating an older guy (she was 19 and he was 26!), and she'd always sneak out to see him at like 4 A.M. It turned out she was dating a teaching assistant—she had to keep it a secret because it could have gotten him fired! But of course people found out. It definitely gave her a reputation.

–Kelsey,
Skidmore College

PUBLIC HOOKUPS!

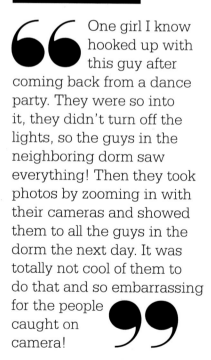

One girl I know hooked up with this guy after coming back from a dance party. They were so into it, they didn't turn off the lights, so the guys in the neighboring dorm saw everything! Then they took photos by zooming in with their cameras and showed them to all the guys in the dorm the next day. It was totally not cool of them to do that and so embarrassing for the people caught on camera!

–Katie, University
of Pennsylvania

TABLE DANCING!

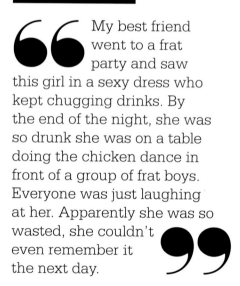

My best friend went to a frat party and saw this girl in a sexy dress who kept chugging drinks. By the end of the night, she was so drunk she was on a table doing the chicken dance in front of a group of frat boys. Everyone was just laughing at her. Apparently she was so wasted, she couldn't even remember it the next day.

–Renae, New York
University

STAY RUMOR-FREE!

These smart moves will keep you from being the next college scandal.

STOP GOSSIPING

When you spread rumors about other people, they won't think twice about airing your dirty laundry.

CLEAN OUT YOUR CONTACTS

Don't keep phone numbers of old hookups in your phone—lots of scandals start with regrettable late-night texts!

BUDDY UP

Go to parties with a friend and keep an eye on each other—just in case the chicken dance sounds like a good idea at 3 A.M.!

LIMIT YOUR LIST

Keep your Facebook, Twitter, and Instagram off the "public" setting so embarrassing pics stay private!

what sex is REALLY LIKE in college

Is everyone doing it? What do guys expect? And will other people judge you for hooking up? Girls fill you in on getting busy in the dorms.

THE BOUNDARIES ARE DIFFERENT

 I used to think 'hooking up' meant making out—it can mean having sex. There's an expectation that things move faster in college. One time I brought a guy back to my dorm room to kiss, and he kept saying, 'I'm sleeping in your bed tonight.' I had no problem telling him no, but it made me realize that guys always assume sex is an option. Know what you want beforehand, so you can put the brakes on if you need to.

—Berkley, University of Mary Washington

THE FREEDOM IS FUN

In college, there are no rules, no curfew, no parents—you make your own decisions, including about sex. With the right guy, that can be exciting and fun! In high school, everyone was judgmental about who was doing it and who wasn't. In college, the pressure of what other people think disappears.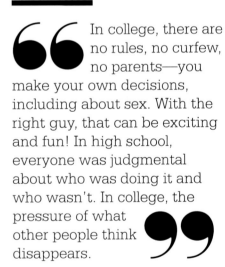

—Kristin, Drake University

HAVING SEX DOES NOT MAKE HIM YOUR BF

In high school, the only people I knew who were having sex were in relationships. In college, no one cares if you sleep with someone you're not dating. What's interesting, though, is that girls react differently to the casualness. Some of my friends think it's exciting to fool around, but some have been crushed when they realize it really was just a one-night stand.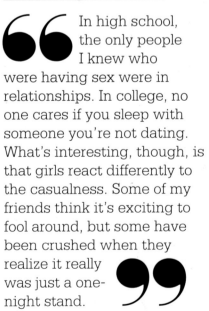

—Melisa, Harvard University

GOING THE *(LONG)*

Your relationship is super-solid right now.

Fact: Moving apart is not going to be a breeze. So if you're already that couple who argues 24-7, the distance will make things even more tense. But if you two are in a good place, you'll both be more likely to make the extra effort that it will take to stay tight.

You stay close with your high school crew.

During the first few months of college, it will feel like there are too many new experiences to explain, which can make you feel as if you don't know each other anymore. But if you're both staying in touch with friends from home, it gives you something to talk about. Plus: Maintaining old friendships takes a new level of maturity—which will help you grow as a couple!

You have lots going on.

That can't-live-without-you love might seem romantic, but the reality is that when your whole life revolves around your guy (and vice versa), it makes being apart extra hard. If you're the type who stays busy with things like your sorority or sports, you won't feel so mopey over not having regular dates. And when you two do talk, you'll have fun stuff to chat about!

DISTANCE

You can't imagine being with anyone else. But will your LDR last past "Dumpsgiving"?

NOT SO MUCH IF...

You have trust issues.

When that girl from his chem lab would post on his Facebook wall, you'd pretend it was no big deal, but you couldn't stop picturing them flirting over their Bunsen burner. Sound familiar? Imagine how you'll feel when he makes new female friends on campus that you know nothing about. Spending the semester Web-stalking him means you won't be making your own memories.

Your schools are hundreds of miles apart.

Sure, some couples find a way to make long, long distance work. But if there's serious mileage between you two, it's going to be almost impossible to do the couple-y things that make you feel connected. Even if you're chatting regularly, when you don't see each other for months at a time, it's easy to grow apart and not even know it until you see each other at Thanksgiving and realize you haven't talked about anything real in forever.

TAKE HER ADVICE!

"Your guy is going to live (and party!) with tons of cute girls. If you get jealous easily, that could cause drama if you're long distance. It's okay to ask about someone once (like the time a flirty girl posted on my BF's Facebook!), but after that, you have to deal—or end it. Harsh but true!"

-Rachel, Barnard College

make your LDR work!

In it for keeps? Here's how to stay together—and still have your own lives—so that your relationship is stronger than ever.

DO...

Get them cleared first! Run it by your roomie that your guy will be around (or you'll all feel tension crammed in your dorm room).

Introduce him to your new BFFs—and let him know who everyone is in your Instagram pics, so he "gets" your new life!

Set up a breakfast phone date for Sunday mornings—you can talk about your weekends, and actually hear each other's voices rather than just texting.

DON'T...

DURING VISITS

Forget about class. Plan trips early in the semester or after midterms, when the workload is light.

MEETING NEW PEOPLE

Pretend that it's okay to date new "friends." Some couples stay together but agree to have an open relationship. In the end, you'll both get hurt.

KEEPING IN TOUCH

Spend all your weekends on Skype. It's normal to miss each other, but it would be way worse to miss out on college because you're wishing you were together.

get through a

"When I went through a breakup, I realized that I had more true friends on campus than I'd thought. I just had to give them a chance to be there for me!"

–Jenna, American University

"After it's over, the most important thing is to go out, be social, and hang out with your friends. Wallowing about your breakup will only hold you back. Do what you have to do to make sure that you are happy and pushing your life forward."

–Mary Elise, Trinity University

"It can be really hard when you see your ex on campus with another girl. College relationships are deeper— so you get close. I ended up calling him and saying a bunch of things I regretted. After that, I decided to be friendly when I saw him on campus. You can't let a past relationship consume you—he's an ex for a reason!"

–Tamika, Howard University

BREAKUP!

new guys, you don't have to watch *The Notebook* on repeat to feel better.

"Over Thanksgiving break, tons of people break up with their high school boyfriend or girlfriend. It isn't easy, but **it's more important to be honest than to string him along.** A friend of mine stayed with his GF for all of freshman year, and it just made it more painful when they eventually broke up."

–Divya, Boston University

"*I coped with a rough breakup by going out to more parties than I should have, and I ended up feeling worse. My friends helped me see that partying wasn't going to make things better and I had to find myself again. I eventually saw that no relationship is worth missing out on being the happiest version of myself.*"

–Allie, Albright College

"I dealt with my first split in college by making a breakup playlist and hanging inspiration quotes on my wall. Hey, whatever it takes!"

–Kerry, Fordham University

"Give yourself an actual *break* from your ex. After that, if you want to be friends, fine. But do not hook up. It's the in-between stuff that causes disasters."

–Michelle, University of Wisconsin-Madison

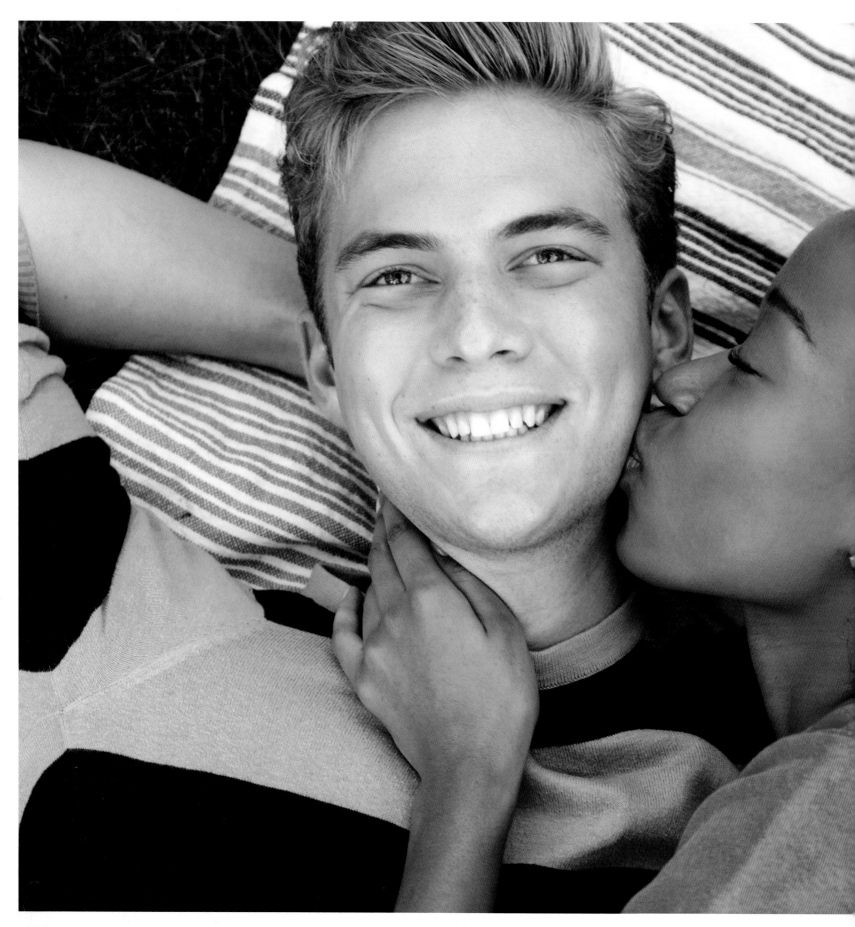

THE GOOD NEWS:
there are lots of sweet guys in college!

Whether you're looking for a hookup, a boyfriend, or a guy just to hang out with, these are the truths—and myths!—about what you can expect.

TRUTH!
THEY DON'T CARE IF YOU'RE POPULAR

"Colleges are big, so there's a wider range of personalities and it's less cliquey than high school. If you're friendly, you'll have no problem meeting guys."

–Caitlin, Indiana University

MYTH!
THEY'RE NOT INTERESTING

"You automatically have something in common because you chose the same school, and the guys are independent and more driven."

–Kathryn, SUNY Purchase

MYTH!
THEY DON'T RESPECT YOUR BRAIN

"It's okay to be into your classes—the good guys want a girl who's smart. They like it when you can work hard and have fun."

–Jenny, Syracuse University

TRUTH!
THEY'RE A LOT FLIRTIER

"Maybe it's because they're out of high school, or maybe it's because they have a blank slate—but college boys tell you straight out how they feel."

–Hannah, University of Notre Dame

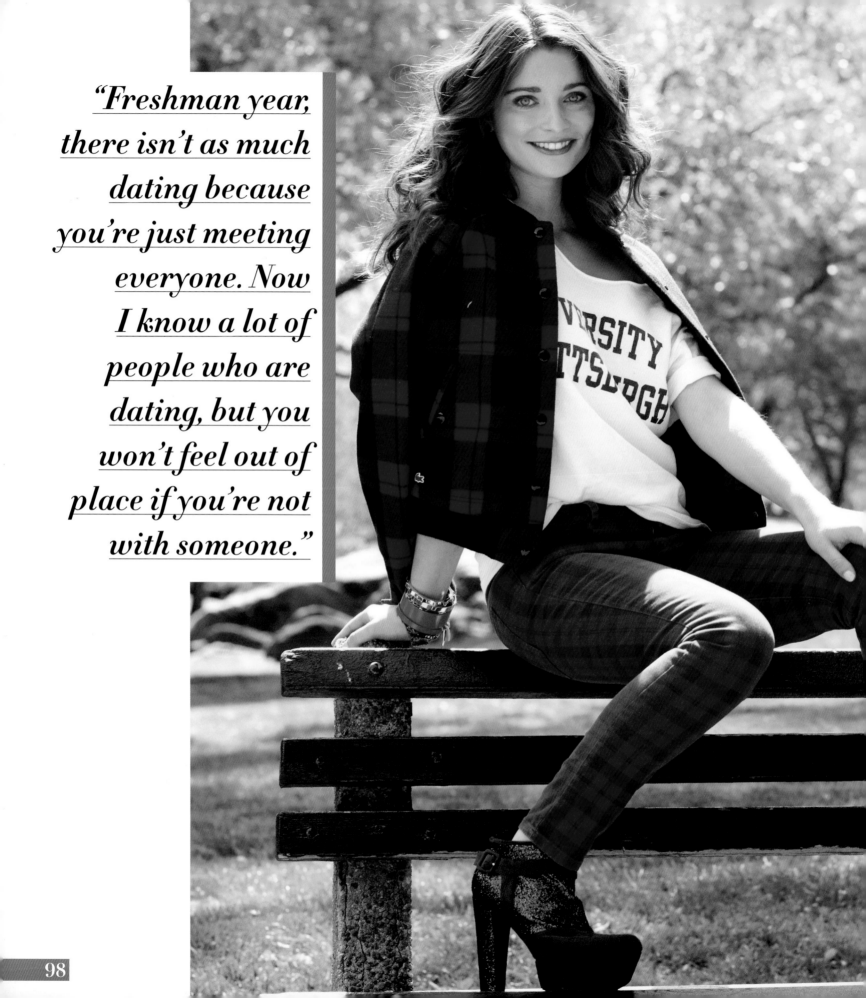

"Freshman year, there isn't as much dating because you're just meeting everyone. Now I know a lot of people who are dating, but you won't feel out of place if you're not with someone."

ASK AN INSIDER!

Claire Peltier, University of Pittsburgh

MAJOR:
Nonfiction writing and communication.

FAVORITE CAMPUS EVENT:
The basketball home opener. Our stadium has one of the most energetic student sections in the country!

DORM STYLE:
Black-and-white modern.

I'M SO GLAD I PACKED:
Flip-flops for the shower. When you're sharing a bathroom with your whole floor, you need something on your feet!

FAVORITE LATE-NIGHT SNACK:
Pretzels and hummus.

BEST TEXT I GOT FROM A COLLEGE GUY:
It was actually my close guy friend—he texted me once to reassure me that he always had my back. (Aw!)

BIGGEST COLLEGE SPLURGE:
I studied abroad in Australia for a semester and then traveled around the country. It was expensive but worth it!

TOP MUSIC TO STUDY TO:
Bon Iver—he has a 25-minute live session that I like to YouTube all the time.

GO-TO OUTFIT FOR PARTIES:
Dark jeans, a pretty tank, and a leather jacket.

ON-CAMPUS LOOK:
Laid-back—but with an edge. When you're comfortable and fashionable, you'll stand out more than a girl who's trying too hard.

INTERNSHIP:
I work at an online fashion magazine. It's great experience!

PARTY
TIME!

college after hours

Everyone knows that a major part of what makes the college experience so awesome is the social scene—whether that means partying in your dorm, dancing with cute guys at a frat house, or throwing a party of your own with your sorority sisters. Here's what to expect when class is over and it's time to have some fun!

it's friday night...
WHERE TO?

Forget lecture halls and lab groups! College girls say they like to let loose at these spots.

A HOUSE PARTY!

" At New York City colleges, everyone lives in a dorm or an apartment and parties out at the bars. So when my friend texted about her guy friend's house party in Brooklyn, I was psyched for a more low-key night out. I convinced my dormmates to make the hour-plus subway trek; and when we got there, the place was crawling with straight boys—a rarity at FIT! After spending so much time with the same kids on campus, it was cool to meet new people. "

—Katie, Fashion Institute of Technology

YOUR DORM!

" One night, I invited a few friends from my photo club to my room for girls' night! We did manis and facials while watching scary movies and—of course—gossiping about the boys in our club! Plus, we had a dorky photo shoot. We'd hung out only in the photo club before, so this gave us a chance to bond in a different way— and now we're super-tight! "

—Ally, Savannah College of Art and Design

THE CLUB!

" I'd never been to a club before, so when my roommate planned a Friday night out dancing with friends, I was in. We tried on tons of dresses and made a guy in our dorm take a gazillion pics of us! When we got to the club at 11 P.M., it was packed with cute boys, and we danced for hours. (Thankfully, we'd all worn flats!) I wasn't sure if clubbing would be my 'thing,' but it totally is—I had a blast with my friends, and it was such a fun way to relax after a full day of classes! "

—Megan, Central Connecticut State University

college party

#1

Drinks are safe as long as you're at a party where you know people.

TRUTH: You never know who is going to be at any given event, so always pour your own drink and never put it down. That way, you'll know what's in it—and that no one has added any sketchy drugs to it (which is a real danger).

#2

Only Greeks have big parties.

TRUTH: You can have tons of fun without pledging a sorority—there will always be plenty of hot parties that are open to everyone in dorms and at off-campus houses.

#3

You have to get invited to parties.

TRUTH:

If you hear about a big party, consider that your invite! College is super-casual and there's no such thing as a formal invite to a house party—so grab your girls and go! Of course, if it's a smaller gathering (like a sorority party for only the girls who belong), you don't want to crash that. But anything else is totally fair game.

MYTHS

You've heard the rumors—now here is the truth behind six major lies to make you feel better before your first night on campus.

#4
Parties are the highlight of the weekend.

TRUTH:

The preparty can be the best part of the night! Invite all your girls to get ready together in your dorm room—blasting tunes and doing makeup can be *more* fun than the main event.

#5
Every night is a party.

TRUTH:

It's true there's always something going on, but most people go out just a few times a week— and spend other nights studying or hanging out. Thursday is a popular party night, but not too many people are getting crazy Sunday through Wednesday!

#6
You'll be left out if you aren't drinking.

TRUTH:

Not every party is a booze fest—there are tons of activities and events that are alcohol-free. Check your student Web site for school-sponsored parties, which are an awesome way to meet new friends!

TAKE HER ADVICE!

"When I was in high school, my motto was 'The bigger the bag, the better.' But college parties take place in a crowded dorm room or a cramped club, so you want just the necessities— aka P-MILK. It's all you need for the night out!"

-Amber, Rider University

REMEMBER YOUR
P-MILK

Ditch your day bag and stuff these five things into a cute clutch or your pocket before heading out!

(**P**) PHONE

(**M**) MONEY

(**I**) ID

(**L**) LIP GLOSS

(**K**) KEYS

10 RULES OF college parties

What to wear and bring, no matter what your scene is—plus other insider info!

1 Don't get too dressed up.

"Most parties are laid-back, so opt for a cute T-shirt, skinny jeans, and flats. You'll look hot—but not like you're trying too hard."

—Leceeon, University of Akron

2 Have backup plans!

"A lot of the time, you'll find a party that's either lame, too crowded, or not your scene. If you know where to go next, you'll never waste time standing around wondering what else is going on!"

—Megan, Central Connecticut State University

3 Stuff a few tissues in your pocket before you head out.

"Big parties run out of toilet paper, so go to the bathroom before you leave your dorm—or put a travel pack of tissues in your purse!"

—Lauren, DePaul University

4 Food will always get you in.

"College students generally don't keep much food in their dorm rooms—so if you show up to a dorm party with a bag of Oreos or chips to share, people will love you forever."

—Holly, Purdue University

5 Wear sleeveless tops to parties—even in winter.

"It might be freezing out, but parties are always packed and it gets really hot!"

—Carolyn, *Pennsylvania State University*

6 Invite a friend from another dorm.

"Dorm parties fill up fast, so bring one good friend who lives somewhere else on campus. That way, everyone gets to meet new people—and she can return the favor and take you to one of her parties!"

—Dawn, *University of Arizona*

7 Plan first if you're going off campus.

"Never go to a party you can't walk to unless you know you have a ride back. It's not worth ending up stranded or in an uncomfortable situation!"

—Brenda, *University of Missouri-Columbia*

8 Use your network.

"If you're going to a frat party, find someone who has friends in that frat—if you have connections, they'll arrange for their pledges to pick you up. This is the best thing about frat parties. I love not having to walk!"

—Casey, *Indiana University*

9 Go all out for theme parties.

"People will compliment you endlessly if you get creative. But don't wear face paint—when the party gets crowded, it will melt right off!"

—Mary, *University of Florida*

10 Leave your heels at home.

"It can take 20 minutes or more to walk across campus, so now I rock flats. Or if I really want to wear heels, I'll throw flip-flops in my bag, just in case!"

—Omawumi, *Georgia State University*

THURSDAY
is the new saturday!

In high school, Friday was the official start of the weekend. In college, most girls squeeze in one extra night of fun. Use these tips to take advantage!

TIP #1
It's no fun to go out when you're stressed! Plan to get your school stuff done on Wednesday, so you can party totally guilt-free on Thursday.

TIP #2
Pick Friday classes that don't start before noon. Even if you're out until 2 A.M. the night before, you can still squeeze in at least eight hours of sleep!

TIP #3
Don't skip class. You might be so wiped out, you'll sleep through the lecture, but drag your butt there anyway. Once you start skipping, you won't be able to stop!

TIP #4
Be selective! On any Thursday night, there will be several parties going on—but you only need to go to the one where you'll think you'll have the best time!

HOW TO GET INTO ANY PARTY

In high school, all it took to get into a party was a working cell phone. But in college, you'll need a few tricks up your sleeve.

SHOW UP IN THE FIRST HOUR

Most college parties start at 10 P.M., so arrive by 11 P.M. to beat the crowd—or risk waiting in line just to get in.

GO OUT WITH YOUR GIRLS

At parties, guys won't hit on you if they think you're taken, so leave your guy friends back at the dorm. (Some frats won't even let you in with dudes!)

KEEP YOUR CREW SMALL

Head out with just a few girls—not your whole floor. That way, you won't stand out as a newbie—freshmen are notorious for partying in packs!

IMPRESS anyone

You're at the party . . . now what? This is how to strike up a convo

"Know the language. You won't look lost talking to upperclassmen if you know that a 'frat star' is the bro who lives for his frat or a 'jersey chaser' is a girl who only hooks up with athletes!"

—Tiffany, University of California, Los Angeles

"Try not to take it personally if someone doesn't recognize you! I met a cute guy late one night, but when I said hi to him on campus a few days later, he stared at me, clueless. Instead of making it a big deal, I just reintroduced myself."

—Blake, George Mason University

"It might sound cheesy, but try **a funny icebreaker!** If you go up to a group where you don't know anyone, say something like, 'I feel like **Lindsay Lohan in** *Mean Girls* on her first day of high school. Mind if I sit with you? I won't put you in my burn book, I promise.' Sometimes just saying hi feels too lame!"

—Kristin, Pennsylvania State University

you talk to!

with anybody—including that cutie from your philosophy class!

"Don't try too hard! I'm from Texas, and the first time my new Cali friends wanted to go to the beach, **I got so dressed up—makeup and all.** Everybody else just grabbed a shirt and shorts! (Cringe.) Now I realize that it's better to just let people see the real you."

-Lindsey, *University of Southern California*

"Cute dudes are everywhere—don't wait for them to come to you! My secret to approaching hot guys is to show interest, but not in an I-stalked-you-on-Facebook-and-Instagram way! I ask him about something he wouldn't post (like his favorite chill spot on campus) to spark a real connection."

-Cici, *University of Nevada, Las Vegas*

"Show off your style! A killer LBD works for any party, and you can't go wrong throwing a denim or camo jacket over whatever you're wearing."

-Lauren, *Ryerson University*

"Be in the moment! It's easy to talk about how much fun you had with your BFFs from home, but that kills the vibe. Stay focused on how excited you are to be in college! Awesome new memories will come naturally."

-Sarah, *Northern Kentucky University*

WHAT HE REALLY NOTICES
about you at a party

Catch his eye in two secs and he won't even realize you were trying.

YOUR SMILE
If you're smiling, he'll think you are more approachable and will be drawn in, so the flirting can begin!

YOUR FRIENDS
His attention will go straight to the group laughing. If you want him to join, stick with two to three pals. (Any more will intimidate him!)

YOUR POSE
Standing up straight shows that you're confident! (Guys dig that.) But don't overthink. If you're relaxed, you'll look it.

YOUR MOVES
Dance—even if you feel silly. If he sees you're having a total blast, he'll want to join in the fun.

"When I'm at a party, I immediately look for a girl who's confident. It says a lot if she's just having fun and not worried about what other people think."

-Michael, Marist College

117

FRAT-PARTY primer

Want to know what to expect from your first on-campus bash? College girls from around the country made this cheat sheet for you!

DO...

DRESS SMART
"Look cute—but don't wear nice shoes. The floors at frats are usually wet, dirty, and covered in sticky beer. Gross!" *-Mia, Trinity College*

GRAB FOOD FIRST
"Eat a late dinner. Parties usually don't start until 11 P.M., and the chance of real food at a frat party is a joke!" *-Ramona, Syracuse University*

KEEP AN OPEN MIND
"Don't skip a party because you've heard negative stuff about the guys. Every group has good and bad members!" *-Monaza, Cal Poly Pomona*

DON'T...

GO TOO SEXY
"At theme parties, most girls dress trashy. But keep it classy if you want to rush a sorority or the older girls will judge." *-Ashley, Rollins College*

DRINK THE JUNGLE JUICE
"It's not juice! Lots of guys won't say what's in it, but usually it's so sugary, you can't taste all the alcohol in it!" *-Yesmel, Rutgers University*

TAKE IT UPSTAIRS
"It's okay to make out on the dance floor—most people are too busy to care—but don't go up to his room." *-Dina, Vanderbilt University*

YOUR GO-TO OUTFIT

YOUR PARTY FUEL

YOUR GUY STRATEGY

PARTY TIPS to live by

We won't call it a *science*, but there are rules to going out! Steal these survival secrets before heading out to a party on campus.

GETTING READY

- Carry a wristlet or small bag you won't have to put down (someone could swipe it, or you could forget it!), and bring only the essentials.

- Take it easy on the eyeliner, or after a night of dancing and partying, all that smoky eye makeup will have you looking like a hot mess.

GOING OUT

- Pick one friend to check in with all night. Make a pact to look out for one another so you won't get stranded in sketchy situations.

- Go to a different place every night out for the first few weeks— you'll meet the most people by switching scenes in the beginning.

COMING HOME

- Wash your face! Otherwise, you'll break out. Plus, now that you're doing your own laundry, you don't want makeup on your pillowcase!

- Wait at least a day before posting Facebook pictures. You might decide the best thing is to delete them!

how to handle
ANY SITCH

You might be tempted to be that crazy party girl in everyone's photos—but nobody likes it when someone is out of control. Find out how to handle any situation before you hit the scene.

THE SITCH

You're being pressured to drink.

You're at a party when upperclassman guys ask you and your friends to chug a beer or take shots with them. When you say no, they start chanting *freshman* over and over until you feel silly.

That beer pong game is making you woozy.

Games like beer pong and flip cup seem fun, but you get so caught up in playing that you don't realize you're sucking down scary amounts of booze. It's not fun or safe to chug your drink until you pass out.

Your friend is always getting wasted.

Most people don't want to stop after just a few beers—and sometimes, the person who overdoes it might be your roommate or BFF. You want to dance and have a good time, but instead you find yourself in the frat bathroom holding her hair back.

A drunk girl is doing shots with your crush.

There are always girls who flirt by taking shots, showing off at beer pong or drinking a ton. While those girls might get attention, they also might get a rep for being party girls. And then that's the only way people see them.

THE FIX

SHRUG IT OFF!

Just let the moment pass. Yeah, sometimes it seems as if you're the only one who's not getting wasted—but if you don't make a big deal of it, no one else will. (Besides, do you really care about impressing guys who act like that?)

MAKE YOUR OWN FUN.

You don't need to join a game to join the party. Introduce yourself to new people, snap photos, or man the iPod. You'll never feel like an outsider when you're having a blast.

DON'T BE THE GO-TO BABYSITTER!

Girls on a mission to get wasted need a friend to make sure they get home safely—but it doesn't *always* have to be you. Sometimes it's okay to skip out on parties with her and get pizza with less wild friends.

IGNORE IT.

You don't need a drink to be sexy. In fact, lots of guys say it's unattractive when girls pound drink after drink—getting sloppy seems trashy.

why college is better SOBER!

You can work the party scene without drinking. Here are five seriously good reasons to skip the booze—and *still* have a blast!

YOUR BODY WILL THANK YOU

Most college kids drink to get drunk—and think that's the only way to have fun. But when a friend throws up in the toilet you use every day because she's so wasted, it's just gross. By staying sober, you don't have to worry about alcohol poisoning, hangovers, or a beer gut!

GUYS WILL NOTICE YOU

Guys are impressed by confidence—not a girl who needs to suck down a six-pack just to relax. Sure, there are *some* guys who just want to get wasted and hang out with people who do the same, but most of them will think it's cool that you have the guts to do your own thing.

YOU'LL HAVE SHARPER RADAR

When you're drinking, it's not always easy to see through people's actions—like when that creepy guy pulls you out onto the dance floor. When you're sober, your guard will go up immediately, potentially saving you from an iffy situation.

YOU'LL REMEMBER WHAT YOU DID

Some girls might think it's cool to brag about how blackout drunk they got, but in reality, there's nothing fun (or safe) about drinking so much that you don't know what you're saying or doing. When you party sober, you'll never have to be that girl who asks around to find out what embarrassing things she did the night before or begs her friends to de-tag her in humiliating Facebook photos.

PEOPLE WILL RESPECT YOU

Staying sober sets you apart from most girls in a good way. You'll never skip class because of a hangover, so teachers will know you take school seriously. And your friends will know they can count on you not to ditch them when you all go out together and *they* are drinking.

HOW TO TURN DOWN A DRINK

(without feeling like a dork!)

"I choose not to drink, so I can stay in control of myself and my actions. When I'm offered a drink, I casually say, 'No thanks,' and move on. People are surprised I don't drink because I'm always having so much fun at parties and clubs. And it has worked to my advantage with guys too—they think it's cool that I don't drink, and they like that they end up drinking less when they're around me."

—Alyssa, *Stanford University*

should you join a SORORITY?

Dozens of BFFs aren't all that come with Greek life. Ask yourself these questions before you decide if rushing is right for you.

Brenda, University of Missouri:

CAN I AFFORD IT?

"During rush, I learned that dues—which cover meals, upkeep on the sorority house, and social events—can be up to $3,000 a year! On top of that, you have to pay for trips and clothes with your sorority letters on them."

AM I WILLING TO GO OUT OF MY COMFORT ZONE?

"Lining up guys for all the social events is so stressful—especially early on, when you don't know anyone on campus! A lot of times, inviting a guy comes with the added pressure to hook up, so girls end up bringing high school friends or even their roommates for drama-free fun."

Jennifer, University of Central Florida:

DO I HAVE TIME?

"During initiation week, I spent more than 24 hours doing sorority stuff, like paddle-decorating and chapter meetings. Now it's more like seven hours a week—but even that feels like a lot. Recently, one of my sisters had her 21st birthday party the night before my exam. Of course, I went . . . and then had to stay up until 3 A.M. to finish studying."

CAN I DEAL WITH THE HATERS?

"People say that sorority girls are slutty and party all the time, but a lot of my sisters have long-term boyfriends and don't drink, just like me. One comment I hate is that I'm 'paying for friends.' Going Greek doesn't mean I'm incapable of making friends on my own; it's just a quicker, more fun way to do it!"

THE PERKS
of pledging

From the outside, it might look as if sororities are all about parties, but there are way bigger benefits than fun formals!

BUILT-IN BENEFITS

Your sisters not only hook you up with dates, but they also help you make connections with fraternity guys through parties known as "swaps." And if you live in the sorority house, you'll enjoy comforts you wouldn't even get at home, like a hired cook!

COMMUNITY SERVICE

The 26 major sororities in the US are overseen by the National Panhellenic Conference, which promotes self-esteem, alcohol screening, and eating-disorder programs and provides $2.8 million in academic scholarships each year. It also encourages sororities to volunteer and fund-raise—so you get to bond with your sisters and feel good about helping others. Bonus: All that community service looks great on your résumé!

NETWORKING OPPS

Because you're a member of a sorority for life, one of the perks is that you can count on the alumni network to help you find jobs and internships. Some of the most powerful women in America, like Condoleezza Rice and Katie Couric, were in a sorority.

SISTER ♥

"I live in the Pi Beta Phi house, and I know that all 129 girls in our chapter would be there for me in a heartbeat. We have amazing times at formals and hayrides and team up with frats for parties, but it's the little things that bond us. We read to kids biweekly, rent out a movie theater and eat popcorn in our pajamas, or have TV nights. My sorority is exclusive—we pick girls who meet high moral standards—but it's for a reason. I would never want someone to join and feel like she didn't belong. Not everyone finds her place in a sorority, but it's so worth it if you do."

—Allison, Ohio University

what RUSH WEEK

Whether you're into sororities or not, it's hard not to wonder what pledgir

IF YOU RUSH, YOU DON'T HAVE TO JOIN

Just because you rush—which is when you have scheduled visits with different sororities in hopes of getting asked to join one—doesn't mean you're obligated to sign up. So even if you're unsure about whether you see yourself in a sorority, you can give it a try.

THERE'S NO ALCOHOL

Rush might seem like one big party, but it's actually very structured: You're at each sorority house for about 20 to 60 minutes, and tons of girls talk to you. There's no alcohol involved—sororities can actually get kicked off campus for serving it—which means you get to see where you click for real, not just when people are buzzed.

THE GIRLS ARE DIVERSE

You might assume the stereotype about sorority girls is true: They are superficial and spend their time gushing over frat guys. Keep an open mind—not every house will be for you, but you might meet some cool, unique people and surprise yourself!

IT *IS* EXPENSIVE

Sororities can cost hundreds of dollars per semester, but the dues usually include a meal plan and keeping the sorority house clean (a bonus if you opt to live there!).

is *really* like

is like. Check out four surprising truths about rush week.

"WHY I'M NOT RUSHING"

These girls decided sorority life wasn't for them—here's why.

"I want to learn more about myself and my interests instead of just following a big group. If I were in a sorority, I feel like I'd spend all my time trying to belong instead of trying to figure out the real me!"

—*Chloe, DePaul University*

"Maybe at a big school where it's hard to find your niche, a sorority would be more useful. But I go to a small school—there's no feeling of getting lost in the crowd."

—*Jessica, University of San Diego*

"Huge groups of girls can be catty. I've heard stories about girls who rub one sister the wrong way and the whole world turns against them. No thanks!"

—*Alex, University of South Carolina*

"*Ditch the heels! I'm almost always in flats now—even if they're not trendy. It's much easier to have fun at parties when your feet aren't aching!*"

ASK AN INSIDER!

Connie Tsang, New York University

MAJOR:
Art history, critical theory, and film.

LATE-NIGHT SNACK:
Take-out dumplings. That's the great thing about a city school—there are so many options to grab a quick bite. I never go to the cafeteria!

MOST LIKELY TO CRUSH ON:
Long-haired literary types. Just like my boyfriend!

BEST STUDY MUSIC:
Classical—I love Bach's cello suite.

FAVORITE PLACE TO HANG OUT:
The coffee shop down the street.

TRICK TO GET A GUY'S ATTENTION AT A PARTY:
Just be yourself and let him impress you. If you can have a good conversation, that's what really counts.

FUTURE DREAM JOB:
Filmmaker.

GO-TO DATE OUTFIT:
A short dress and ankle boots, or I edge it up with some leather pants.

MONEY SPENT PER MONTH ON COFFEE:
$20.

MONEY SPENT PER MONTH ON CLOTHES:
Ah, way too much! Living in the city is expensive. I try to keep my going-out budget to $250 a month, but it's hard.

FAVORITE THEME-PARTY COSTUME:
Robots. I'm serious!

BEST TEXT I GOT FROM A COLLEGE GUY:
When we first started dating, my boyfriend used to send me poems by Lord Byron every night. We go to different schools, so it was a cute way to stay in touch.

STRETCH YOUR $$$ ON CAMPUS

make and save $$$ at college!

Now that you're living on your own, it's true that you need to be a *little* more careful about your cash flow—especially if you want to have enough left over after expenses to pay for that cute new pair of jeans, pizza delivery, and an unforgettable spring break with your new BFFs. The good news: It's totally doable if you set a budget and get a bit creative! Here's how to make—and save!—money for the next four years, so you can enjoy every second of college life.

4 SCHOLARSHIP SECRETS nobody told you

Score serious cash, so the only thing you'll have to stress over this semester will be what to wear to that theme party.

1. TALK TO WINNERS

At **thecollegeninja.com**, scholarship winners share how they found big money to cover college tuition and expenses. You can ask questions, bounce scholarship application essays off them, and more!

2. EXPLORE LOCAL OPTIONS

Organizations like the Rotary Club, Elks Foundation, and churches often offer money to students. Track down leads by asking your parents' friends, community business owners, and that family near campus you occasionally babysit for!

3. USE YOUR PASSION

Whatever makes you *you* could mean free cash. For example, if you're vegetarian, apply for the Vegetarian Resource Group Scholarship next year! Into zombies? **Scholarshipexperts.com** offers a $1,500 award for a killer zombie-apocalypse escape plan. (Seriously!) Check out **mycollegedollars .com**—it syncs up with your Facebook profile and matches you to scholarships.

4. ENTER NATIONAL CONTESTS

Huge awards from companies like Coca-Cola and Best Buy can seem out of reach, but *someone* has to win: A girl once scored $20,000 for writing a funny tweet in KFC's Colonel's Scholars Contest! That's a lot of money for 140 characters or fewer.

STRETCH YOUR summer dollars

You didn't just sit on the beach this year—you were all about making money before leaving for campus! Use these tricks from college girls, so your extra cash lasts through second semester.

USE THE "222" RULE

" Whenever I am tempted to buy something that's more than $30, I ask, Will I care about this in two weeks? Two months? Two years? If I don't answer yes to all three Qs, it's a no-go. I worked too hard at my part-time job to blow my cash. I've saved almost $800! "

–Aubrey, Drexel University

SAVE $1 MORE EACH DAY

" On the first day of my part-time job as a United Nations tour guide, I saved $1. Then every day after that, I added one dollar more than the day before. After four months, I saved about $700! Now that's my emergency savings fund! "

–Ashlyn, John Jay College

GIVE YOURSELF AN ALLOWANCE

" Over the summer, I worked one job during the week and another on weekends. I set up direct deposit for my weekday job—those checks went into my savings account. The rest became spending money. I saved enough for room and board and still had money for fun! "

–Meghan, Central Connecticut State University

STASH YOUR SINGLES

" I'm a waitress at school. When I get home from a shift, I put all my single dollar bills in a jar instead of in my wallet. I know I'd be more likely to spend those than break a twenty! "

–Lacey, University of Delaware

5 WAYS
not to go broke

Tuition costs are a monster—but all those little extras can add up, too! See how to live it up on less.

RECYCLE

"Every week, everyone in my dorm collects recyclables, and our RA exchanges them to get money for dorm activities. You could do the same thing at your school. On Sunday morning, there are always tons of cans and bottles left over from the weekend parties!"

—Janessa, University of California, San Diego

USE FREE SCHOOL SUPPLIES

"Instead of buying a printer, refill paper, and ink cartridges, I use the free computer labs on campus. Their laser printers spit out pages super-fast! Plus, printing all the readings I'd need from my dorm room would a) take forever and b) require so much ink. My roommate spends about $50 a month on new black-ink cartridges!"

—Mary, University of Florida

GO TO EVENTS

"You can get free food almost every day if you take advantage of the activities that student groups host. Like every week, my dorm has a 'study break' with pizza. It's fun, you get to see friends, and you won't spend as much as you do in the dining hall!"

—Carolyn, Pennsylvania State University

SIGN UP FOR DEALS

"I have an e-mail account just for mailing lists from all my favorite stores—so I get exclusive coupons and always know about special sales. I don't remember the last time I actually paid full price for something!"

—Lauren, DePaul University

BUY BOOKS ONLINE

"I never knew college books cost so much—I spent $500 my first semester! Now I use sites like **chegg.com** or **amazon.com** to rent the books I need at way cheaper prices. I found a Spanish book that normally costs $100 for just $15."

—Anique, Howard University

BUDGET
your money

What will you spend? Check out what one real student spent in a week, so you can see what *your* budget might be like!

MONDAY
coffee: $2.50
lunch: $10
admission to party: $5

TUESDAY
breakfast smoothie $3.75
sorority movie night: $8.25

WEDNESDAY
printing English project: $4.35
sandwich: $7.50
T-shirt from campus store: $9.25

THURSDAY
lunch at the burger shop: $6.80
groceries: $33.78
coffee at the library: $3

FRIDAY
magazines: $5
lunch on the quad: $7
night out with the girls: $15

SATURDAY
Forever 21 purchase: $27.05
variety-show tickets: $5.50
toga party: $11.50

SUNDAY
IHOP breakfast: $8.60
dinner at Panera: $9.75
book for bio class: $45

WEEKLY TOTAL:
$228.58

PUT YOUR CREDIT CARD AWAY!

"When I got to college, I found myself putting everything on my credit card: shopping trips, gas, food. I figured I'd somehow come up with a way to deal with the bills later, but by the end of sophomore year, I was a few thousand dollars in debt. It's easy to see credit cards as free money, so now I pay in cash so I can see what I'm really spending."

–Holly, University of Maryland

SNEAKY money savers!

Find creative ways to cut costs and you'll always have extra dollars in your pocket!

1 Stock up at home.

The next time you're on break, buy a bunch of snacks and goodies to bring back with you. You won't be tempted to eat out as much if you have food nearby—and maybe your parents will pay for it if you ask them to go shopping with you.

2 Keep the change.

Put loose coins in a large jar. You'll be surprised how quickly they add up! It could even pay for your spring-break trip.

3 Get huge discounts.

Buying a Student Advantage Card ($20 at studentadvantage.com) will help you save 10 to 50 percent at retailers like Foot Locker, Topshop, and target.com.

4 Go out for cheap.

Sign up at entertainment.com, and get access to more than 1,000 online coupons for places such as Pizza Hut and your local movie theater.

5 Resell your books.

Don't just let textbooks sit on your shelf when you're done with them. If you bought them at the campus bookstore, return them for a partial refund—it can resell your books to other students. If you bought them online, trade them for other used books at swapbooks.com, or resell them and use the money to buy your reading for next semester!

6 Sign up for a free checking and savings account.

You should never pay monthly fees or charges for online banking, fund transfers, or ATM withdrawals.

7 Head off campus.

Buying things like cleaning supplies at the campus store can cost way more than if you just went to a nearby store like CVS or Target.

8 Pay your bills on time.

Don't get hit with late fees for credit card, cell phone, or utility bills (if you're living off campus). Why pay $125 for something that costs $100? If you can't pay before the due date, call the company to make payment arrangements. Lots of places will cut you a little slack if you just ask.

9 Join the club.

Get a few friends to pitch in for an annual membership at Costco or Sam's Club. Buy groceries, school supplies, toothpaste, soap, and deodorant in bulk, and split the haul.

10 Host a clothes swap.

If you're getting sick of your going-out clothes by second semester, invite a bunch of girl friends over to your dorm and ask everyone to bring three things they're tired of wearing—then trade with each other! You won't spend money shopping, but you'll still walk away with some new outfits.

cash in over
WINTER BREAK

If you're shelling out big-time for everyone on your gift list, follow these tips to earn some cash before you go back to campus!

GOT 2 MINUTES?
SWAP GIFT CARDS!

Relatives can be so off base when it comes to presents. (Um, thanks for the $20 to Talbots?) Trade unwanted gift cards for cash at **giftcardrescue.com**— you'll get back up to 90 percent of the value!

GOT 2 HOURS?
BE A WRAP STAR!

Offer to wrap gifts, trim trees, run errands, or shovel snow for $8–$20 an hour. (Start simple tasks at the low end, and add on for projects that require heavy lifting.) Spread the word by posting on Facebook or putting fliers in neighbors' mailboxes.

GOT 4 HOURS?
GO SHOPPING!

Already snagged the perfect New Year's dress? Keep looking anyway—if you score vintage dresses for cheap from thrift stores, you can wash or dry-clean them and then resell them on eBay or Etsy for up to 10 times what you paid!

GOT A WEEKEND?
MAKE HOUSE CALLS!

Tons of people head out of town for the holidays. If you're not one of them, offer to grab their mail and water their plants for $8 a day, or feed and walk their pets for $10. If they want you to stay overnight to keep an eye on things, bump your rate to about $30!

IT'S A MONEY EMERGENCY!

Need quick cash? Skip weeks of babysitting and try these shortcuts so you can go out with everyone else on your hall!

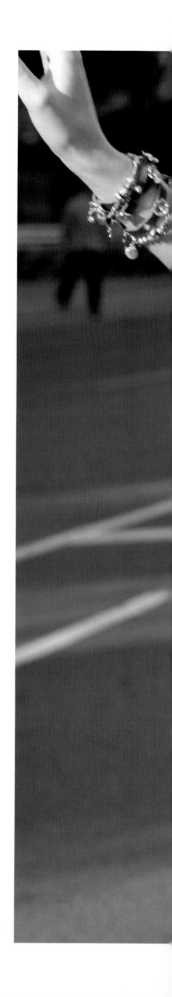

TEACH A LESSON

Cash in on your 4.0 with **wyzant.com**. Here's how it works: You tutor kids in school subjects and test prep over e-mail or Skype right from your dorm room, and you'll net $18–$48 a session. The more hours you log, the more you'll earn.

HAND OUT FLIERS

It might sound old-fashioned, but plenty of businesses still get the word out with fliers—especially near college campuses. Retail stores, coffee shops, and restaurants all need help advertising their business. Plus, it only takes a few hours and you might make new friends!

PIMP YOUR RIDE

Got a car on campus? Use it as a moving billboard! Myfreecar.com sends you stick-ons from sponsors—a small decal gets you $50 a month, while ads that wrap the whole car equal up to $400! Ignore judge-y friends by thinking of all the cash you're banking.

SELL YOUR SKILLS

Promote whatever you're good at on **fiverr.com**, where you can charge $5 to $500 for specialized talents, like designing jewelry or creating company Facebook pages. The site e-mails you when someone wants your product. Ka-ching!

"I work at a restaurant and bar near campus. The extra money helps me do things like get my nails done without feeling bad or asking my parents for money!"

ASK AN INSIDER!

Nilla Ali, University of Virginia

MAJOR:
Economics.

COLLEGE MOTTO:
Take time to breathe and soak in what's happening!

DORM-ROOM STYLE:
Vintage.

MONEY SPENT PER MONTH GOING OUT:
$200.

GO-TO OUTFIT FOR CLASS:
Comfortable leggings and a cute oversize sweater. I like to stand out, but I also like to be comfortable, so layering with statement pieces is always a great way to go.

FAVORITE STUDY SNACK:
Oatmeal. I also keep apples and grapes on hand for late nights.

BEST TEXT FROM A COLLEGE GUY:
"Thinking of you."

WORST TEXT FROM A COLLEGE GUY:
"Who is this?"

BEST PLACE TO MEET GUYS:
The gym, preferably before you're not all sweaty.

I TOTALLY DIDN'T NEED TO PACK:
Books to read for fun. There's enough reading for class!

MOST LIKELY TO CRUSH ON:
The social butterfly.

FAVORITE STUDY SPOT:
Whole Foods—yup, food and coffee at your leisure!

CURE FOR HOMESICKNESS:
Repeat to yourself out loud, "I only get to do this for four years."

TOP THING EVERY COLLEGE GIRL NEEDS IN HER CLOSET:
A fun pair of boots!

BIGGEST COLLEGE SPLURGE:
Spring break in Brazil.

TRICK TO GET A GUY'S ATTENTION IN CLASS:
Forget class! Join his study group, and show off how smart you are.

chapter six

STEP UP YOUR COLLEGE STYLE

make a statement on campus

In high school, you probably wore whatever was popular. And while there's nothing wrong with incorporating trends into your look, in college, you want to do way more than just fit in. Your clothes should say something about *you* . . . even when you're just walking through the quad. But before you can showcase your style, you need to define it. Turn the page to find out how to mix and match your essentials—plus some cute closet extras—to get *your* look.

RULE 1

HAVE A GO-TO OUTFIT

When you oversleep—and you will—reach for fail-safe skinnies and a cozy sweater.

your new FASHION RULES

Now that you're a small fish in a big pond, looking amazing requires a higher degree of fashion smarts. Try these must-have looks to stand out in the best way possible.

RULE 2

OWN A FRACKET

Don't party on fraternity row without a jacket that can withstand any spill—like a faux-leather moto jacket.

RULE 3

A LITTLE SPARKLE GOES A LONG WAY

For a semester's worth of parties, a sequined top is really the only piece you'll need.

RULE 4
BE A JEAN-IOUS
Save your sweats for the gym! When you're just hanging out, a comfy pair of jeans looks less sloppy.

RULE 5
FRIEND SOME FLATS
You'll cross campus more times than you can count. Do it in the flattest, coolest shoes you can find.

RULE 6
GET CARDED
A pretty cardigan cleans up any outfit (and is the perfect protection against freezing lecture halls).

look perfect for EVERY OCCASION!

There are tons of events on and off campus—and you'll want to look great for all of them. These real college students are here to help you get dressed!

RUSH WEEK

POLISHED BLOUSE

"You're essentially interviewing to be in a sorority, so you don't want to seem as if you don't care! A button-down always looks crisp."

DRESS AND FLATS

"For slightly nicer rush events, a girly dress is perfect, and patterned flats keep it from looking over-the-top dressy!"

CROSS-BODY BAG

"You're shaking a lot of hands as you meet people, so it's annoying to have to juggle a purse."

FUN JEANS
"My first night of rush was casual, so jeans were a no-brainer. Stand out by choosing a printed pair!"

"You've got limited time to make an impression on sorority sisters, so you want your personality to shine through your convo— and your clothes!"

—Jessica,
Marist College

GLAM NECKLACE

"It's funky to pair a bold necklace with a rocker tee—I love how unexpected it is!"

"Spring fling is like going to a major concert . . . right on campus! Bring out your rocker side with an edgy outfit."

-Elizabeth, George Washington University

CUTOFF SHORTS

"It's a music event, and ripped shorts in a light wash feel very Woodstock."

164

MUSIC FESTIVAL

COOL JACKET

"If the weather is unpredictable, you'll want a coat to be safe. Leather matches the rock vibe, and if you have the urge to mix it up, throw in a bold print, too!"

EASY SNEAKERS

"You'll be standing all day, so comfy shoes are a must. A plain white pair goes with everything."

GRAPHIC TEE

"A concert is one of the most laid-back events on campus, so a cute vintage-looking tee is perfect!"

CHIC SHADES

"Everyone else will be in aviators, so make a statement in fashion-y sunglasses."

FRAT PARTY

METALLIC SKINNIES

"A shimmery color is such a simple way to make jeans feel special enough for a party."

MINI CLUTCH AND HEELS

"I'm petite, so heels are a must! And a wristlet is perfect because you can slip it on and don't have to worry about losing it."

JEAN JACKET

"Denim goes with everything! Wear it with a fancy dress *or* pants! Plus, it's lightweight and easy to carry around all night."

"Some frat events are formal, so I like to have a standout dress. Lace always looks pretty, and a corset style is really flattering!"

"Obviously there are boys at a frat party, so you want to look fun and flirty! For me, that means going glam."

—Carolyn, *New York University*

DRESS FOR YOUR

University of Alabama

"It's very Southern to dress super-girly for everything! For class, I might even wear a tee with a flirty skirt and heels."

—Abby

PATTERNED MINI

Loyola Marymount University

"Sororities are big here, and this look would be perfect for rush! Mixing femme pieces with a blazer makes a great first impression."

—Amy

University of Texas–Pan American

"I go to school in Texas, where it stays hot into the fall. I wear shorts with layers, so I can stay warm in the classroom and cool outside."

—Sara

BRIGHT SHORTS

George Brown College

"Being experimental with fashion is a thing at my college. So I color-blocked with my shorts and then added sneakers and a fun backpack."

—Catherine

SCHOOL!

If college had fashion rankings, these undergrads would dominate. Let them show you the right way to remix what's in your closet.

Fashion Institute of Technology

"Living in New York, you have to be fashion-forward! For a chic look, I pair trendy graphic bottoms with leather and a red bag."

—Jessica

PRINTED PANTS

Temple University

"On an urban campus, I want people to know I'm friendly! Fun pants and a yellow shirt give you a happy vibe."

—Lauren

Indiana University

"Big campuses have lots going on! A classic skirt and a denim vest walk the line between casual and dressy, so you will be ready for anything."

—Katherine

CIRCLE SKIRT

University of San Francisco

"San Fran style is very diverse! I like to edge up a skirt with boots but add a pink bow to keep it a little sweet."

—Chelsea

don't forget to

Little extras help

floral scarf
A jean-and-tee uniform gets a quick step up with a pretty scarf.

BIG STATE SCHOOL

slick aviators
When it's sunny, these shades are the way to go! Buy two pairs, so if you lose one, you'll have a backup!

chunky watch
These look cool and will help when you are rushing to get to class on time and haven't recharged your phone!

charm necklaces
Layers of delicate charm necklaces make a personal statement—no one's mix looks quite like yours.

retro backpack
These fit everything! Pick one with a cool thrift-store feel.

ART SCHOOL

combat boots
Shoes can make or break an outfit. These boots are functional and fashionable.

ACCESSORIZE!

Transform any outfit! These are the key picks for your type of school.

IVY LEAGUE

unique iPhone case
Everyone has an iPhone—so find a special case to make yours a fashion statement.

a big carryall
It's super-practical—and much sleeker than a bulky backpack.

flat riding boots
These are crazy popular—they look chic and work in any weather.

shoulder bag
The object is to get around the city without looking like a student—this fits all your stuff but blends in!

edgy sneakers
Invest in trendy sneakers, like these wedge ones. Not only do they look cool, but you also could walk the streets all day in them—literally!

CITY SCHOOL

colorful bangles
A stack of these bracelets is an easy way to brighten up any outfit.

TIME TO SHAKE IT UP!

To look chic, you have to take some fashion risks. That means finding ways to reinvent college wardrobe staples!

CLASS UP RIPPED JEANS

SHREDDED DENIM GOES FROM SLOPPY TO SOPHISTICATED WHEN YOU ADD A HALF-TUCKED BUTTON-DOWN AND KILLER SHOES.

GET A LITTLE SPORTY

DON'T SAVE YOUR JERSEY FOR GAME DAY! USE IT FOR A FUN POP OF COLOR UNDER OVERALLS TO WIN MAJOR STYLE POINTS.

GIRL-IFY YOUR SWEATS

Boom! Your chill hangout just got a heck of a lot flirtier with this comfy sweatshirt-and–flippy floral skirt combo.

what to wear to your

You want to start your career off on the right foot. Step one: acing your

CONSERVATIVE

66 I'm interning at a law firm and I need to look buttoned-up, but I don't want to be boring! *99*

—Nicole

☑ **cool classics**
Pick staples (like trousers and collared shirts) in cool prints and textures for a twist on the classic "work" look.

☑ **tuxedo pants**
Dress pants are a must—they make you look instantly professional! Pick ones with stripes down the sides for an added kick of style.

☑ **initial bangle**
Add a little touch of "you" with a monogrammed bracelet.

☑ **gold flats**
If you know you'll be on the go all day, give your feet a break with flats! Pick metallic ones and they won't seem overly casual.

☑ **striped A-line**
This cut won't be too clingy or revealing, and the graphic detail gives it personality.

☑ **structured tote**
A slouchy bag can veer into schlumpy territory. Upgrade to a bag that has a squared shape and enough room to fit all your stuff.

INTERNSHIP

internship outfit! Fit right in, no matter where you're working.

CREATIVE

☑ **mixed colors and prints**
No need to be matchy-matchy! Let your artistic nature show by pairing a cute printed dress with a bag and shoes in different colors.

☑ **novelty knit**
Reveal different sides of your personality by layering a quirky sweater over a femme, flowery button-down.

☑ **printed pants**
Rock the whole casual-Friday thing in floral skinnies, a cardigan, and chic heels.

☑ **bucket bag**
The loose shape and zebra print perfectly fit the casual-cool vibe.

☑ **bold heels**
Show how fashion-y you are with two hot trends in one shoe—color-blocking and a d'Orsay shape.

☑ **metallic skirt**
Make a basic blazer way more exciting with a glittery skirt that will add shine to your whole look!

" I'll be surrounded by clever, cool people at the ad agency where I'm interning. I want to look just as fun and interesting. "

—Brooke

look pretty 24-7

Whether you're hanging with your roommate, sitting in psych class, or hitting a frat party, you always want to put your best face forward— *and* have a #goodhairday! So what makeup look is best for *your* style, and how do you get awesome strands in a hurry? Find out all the answers, plus some real-girl recs for the products you'll be so glad you packed.

pretty little

FOR THE MORNING YOUR ALARM DIDN'T GO OFF

"A thicker-than-usual lip pencil feels velvety when I put it on, not dry. It also gives my lips bright color, so I don't need to wear much other makeup to look chic."

–Maria, junior

FOR GREASY HAIR

"I don't always have time to wash my hair before early lectures. In the past, I've used baby powder to soak up oil, but now I sprinkle on dry shampoo because it doesn't leave my hair looking flaky or white!"

–Rachel, sophomore

FOR THE MORNING AFTER A CRAM SESH

"Dabbing a rosy stain on my cheekbones was all I needed to look fresh and awake. It would be perfect after a long night of studying in the library."

–Courtney, junior

ESSENTIALS

Not sure what makeup to bring? The sisters of Delta Gamma sorority at Pennsylvania State University share their fave products so you can look gorgeous all semester!

FOR SHINY SKIN

"When I'm going from class to class, my face tends to get shiny! An oil-free moisturizer helps it stay matte, even if I'm running around all day."

-Ruby, senior

FOR SHORTS SEASON

"Your roommates will totally try to borrow this shaving cream! When you just use plain soap, your shave isn't as close and your skin can get dry. A silky cream leaves legs satiny and smooth!"

-Courtney, junior

FOR A FLASH FACIAL

"A natural clay mask cleans out my pores and makes my skin so smooth—an absolute *must* before a formal!"

-Madison, junior

FOR A GORGEOUS TIME-OUT

"During study breaks, I love to paint my nails! Mint green is one of my favorite colors, but I like to mix in one or two other shades, too, to make accent nails!"

-Heather, senior

FOR A NIGHT OUT WITH YOUR GIRLS

"I look for mascara with a thick wand and bristles that don't cause clumping! I want every lash coated, so I can look super-glam for a night out with friends."

-Allyson, sophomore

do your makeup in
5 MIN. OR LESS!

No one will ever guess you rolled out of bed and made it to class with only seconds to spare, thanks to these easy looks.

if you're CLASSIC

STEP 1: SKIN

Tinted moisturizer evens out your skin tone faster than you can guzzle a grande latte! It also goes on so smoothly that you don't have to spend time precisely applying it. Dot it on your forehead, nose, and chin, and then blend it out with your fingers.

STEP 2: EYES

Fake wide-awake eyes with face-framing brows and curled lashes. A colorless brow gel is a goofproof way to tame brows in a rush, and a curling mascara means you can skip the hassle of using an actual curler.

STEP 3: LIPS

Swipe on a long-lasting lipstick in an attention-grabbing color (like berry!) and you won't have to reapply all day.

STEP 1: SKIN

Don't waste time with a multistep face-makeup routine—BB cream does it all! Quickly smooth it all over to cover splotchy skin, breakouts, and dark circles.

STEP 2: EYES

Create the fastest smoky eyes ever with a jumbo pencil—just line eyes and smudge outward. Finish with a lash stain. It keeps lashes dark for days and won't wash off in the shower.

STEP 3: LIPS

For a pretty pout that stays moisturized, dab a clear balm on your lips. Since it's colorless, you can do a swift swipe without smearing it.

if you're EDGY

if you're BOHO

STEP 1: BROWS

For an instantly pulled-together look, sketch in brows with a brown pencil and blend with a brow brush.

STEP 2: EYES

Shimmery pink highlighter on your eyes is a shortcut for making them sparkle. Just sweep on a cream formula straight from the tube.

STEP 3: LIPS + CHEEKS

Add a pretty flush to lips and cheeks with a double-duty stain. Use your fingers to apply on the fly.

ACE YOUR

When you've pulled an
ALL-NIGHTER

pink blush
"I can't live without blush! It immediately warms up your face under those harsh lecture-room lights."

tinted BB cream
"The last thing I have time to worry about is my skin! This stuff evens out my skin tone, so I don't look blotchy."

Sarah, a student at the University of Alabama and the blogger behind **toomuchisneverenough .com**, knows how to score that I-swear-I'm-awake face even when you're exhausted.

calming spray
"A spritz cools my face and helps calm my nerves right before an exam."

black mascara
"A big wand makes lashes thicker, which helps eyes look awake after late nights!"

red polish
"For a fun, quick break during an all-nighter, I paint my nails a vivid shade!"

bright lipstick
"A bold color draws attention away from tired eyes!"

face!

In college, you have to be able to switch your look in an instant. These college beauty bloggers share their must-haves for whichever quick makeover you need!

When you're going to A PARTY!

loose curls
"You never want to look like you're trying too hard around hot senior guys. A clampless wand gives you natural-looking curls quickly."

Heading to a party? Swap that casual gloss for some statement lipstick and then some! Katie, a student at the University of California, San Diego, and blogger at thekatizzle.tumblr.com, tells you how to go all out!

metallic polish
"Shimmery colors don't chip as easily, so they last through a Saturday night—even if I paint them during the week!"

portable perfume
"House parties get packed and sweaty! I bring a roller-ball scent to stay fresh."

eyeshadow palette
"I don't have space for lots of shadow pots, so this palette is key. It has all the sparkly shades you need to look chic."

cherry gloss
"Frat bathrooms are gross! To avoid needing to go into one for a touch-up, fill in lips with liner and then dab gloss on top—the color won't budge!"

be the *BEST*

BRAID

FISHTAIL
Look chic all day! Divide hair into two sections. Take a small piece from one section and bring it over to the other section. Repeat until you get to the bottom and secure.

CLASS

PONY

SOFT BOUNCE
No worries if you are too tired after that all-nighter to wash your hair! Second-day (even third-day) hair is made for teasing. Backcomb at the crown, and then gather into a pony.

BUN

EFFORTLESS TOPKNOT
Keep hair out of your face while you're studying by pulling it into a topknot. Smooth down any flyaways with a spritz of hairspray to keep it sleek.

tressed

There are so many opps for good hair moments, whether you're sitting in class or heading out to a party! Let these ideas inspire you.

BUN
FLIRTY KNOT
Look casually cool for a dorm hangout with hallmates by going with an off-center part, loose wavy bangs, and a messy side bun.

PARTY

PONY
BUBBLE PONYTAIL
For a rush event, add fun to a basic pony by wrapping clear elastics around the tail every two inches or so.

BRAID
MOD TWIST
Rock a frat party with a faux hawk! Tease bangs, pin them into a pouf, and reverse French-braid the rest. Just cross the two outer sections under the middle section, rather than over.

PHOTO CREDITS

CHAPTER 3: MASTER THE GUY SCENE

CHAPTER 4: PARTY TIME!

seventeen

Editor-in-Chief **ANN SHOKET**

Creative Director **JESSICA MUSUMECI**

Executive Editor **BETHANY HEITMAN**

Book Design by **WENDY ROBISON**

Text by **CAITLIN MOSCATELLO**

Photo Editor **ANTONELLA D'AGOSTINO**

Assistant Editor **ALEX ABEL**

Copy Editor **MARISA CARROLL**

Project Manager **KARRIE WITKIN**

THANK-YOUS

Sally Abbey, Alison Jurado, Meaghan O'Connor,
Mark Gompertz, Jacqueline Deval,
Chris Navatril, Frances Soo Ping Chow,
Cindy De La Hoz, and the whole Running Press team.